RECLAIMING YOUR
MIDLIFE
Mojo

InspiredLIVING
PUBLISHING

A Sacred Gift to Support You on Your Midlife Journey

Discover the power of energy-infused affirmations to elevate your mindset and create your intentional life.

Mindset Mojo™ *Intentional Life* Screensaver Set

Your Mindset Mojo™ Affirmation Screensaver Set includes:

~5 energy-infused affirmation screensavers for your desktop or laptop

~5 energy-infused affirmation screensavers for your phone

~Invitation to the Inspiration Lounge™ Facebook community

~VIP notice on future complimentary 5-day Mindset Mojo™ Soul Camps

It's time to say yes to igniting your inner mojo and to living an intentional life!

Download your complimentary gift at:
www.MindsetMojoGiftSet.com

Published by Inspired Living Publishing, LLC.
P.O. Box 1149, Lakeville, MA 02347
(508) 265-7929

Print ISBN: 978-1-7327425-6-7
Digital ISBN:978-1-7327425-7-4
Library of Congress Control Number: 2022941333

Cover Design: Mandy Gates, GruveDesign.com
Interior Layout Design: Heather McNamara, yourbrandtherapy.com
Interior Layout: Patricia Creedon, patcreedondesigns.com
Editors: Deborah Kevin, deborahkevin.com
        Jill Celeste, jillceleste.com

Linda Joy photo credit: Ali Rosa Photography, alirosaphotography.com.

Dedication

This book is dedicated to ...

*E*very woman who, in honoring herself and the whispers of the small voice within, bravely said yes to reclaiming her inner mojo--her own unique magic and feminine wisdom.

Every woman who bravely chooses, time and time again, to rise above her fear and self-doubt and to peel back the layers that hide or dim her divine light.

Every woman who lights the way and extends an outstretched hand to uplift, empower, and support other women on their journey. Thank you for being a beacon.

And, also to...

Niki, my loving daughter, and her husband Glenn: One of my greatest joys is watching the two of you co-create a magical life together that envelops Makenna in love, joy, and lots of laughter.

Makenna (aka "The Little Goddess"), my spirited, creative, love-filled eleven-year-old granddaughter: may you always embrace your magic and magnificence, my love, and never dull your sparkle.

Tyler, my grandson: may you remember your truth and magic and find the greatest peace and happiness in that truth.

Dana, my soul mate, best friend, and love of my life: twenty-eight years in, you still make my heart skip a beat, bring a smile to my lips, and make me feel like the most important woman in the world. I'm truly blessed.

To the authors of *Reclaiming Your Midlife Mojo,* who entrusted their sacred stories to me and allowed me to share them with the world. Thank you for such an honor.

The extraordinary team of talented women with whom I have been honored, blessed, and humbled to work with to bring this project to life: Deborah Kevin, editor on this sacred project, who brings the essence of each story to light; Jill Celeste, associate editor; Mandy Gates for the stunning cover and interior design; and Patricia Creedon for the layout; and Kim Turcotte, my Goddess of Operations and soul sister, who, for over a decade, organizes, and brings my visions to life.

And finally, to ...

You, the reader–may these empowering stories of self-discovery, resilience, and transformation remind you of your own truth and power. I am deeply grateful that our paths crossed at this moment and time.

www.InspiredLivingPublishing.com

Inspired Living Publishing's bestselling titles include:

The Art of Self-Nurturing: A Field Guide to Living with More Peace, Joy & Meaning
by Kelley Grimes, MSW

Broken Open: Embracing Heartache and Betrayal as Gateways to Unconditional Love
by Mal Duane

Soul-Hearted Living: A Year of Sacred Reflections & Affirmations for Women by Dr. Debra Reble

Everything Is Going to Be Okay!: From the Projects to Harvard to Freedom by Dr. Catherine Hayes, CPCC

Being Love: How Loving Yourself Creates Ripples of Transformation in Your Relationship and the World by Dr. Debra Reble

Awakening to Life: Your Sacred Guide to Consciously Creating a Life of Purpose, Magic, and Miracles by Patricia Young

The Art of Inspiration: An Editor's Guide to Writing Powerful, Effective Inspirational & Personal Development Books
by Bryna Haynes.

As well as these bestselling titles in our sacred anthology division:

Life Reimagined: Women's Stories of Hope, Resilience and Transformation

SHINE! Stories to Inspire You to Dream Big, Fear Less & Blaze Your Own Trail

Courageous Hearts: Soul-Nourishing Stories to Inspire You to Embrace Your Fears and Follow Your Dreams

Midlife Transformation: Redefining Life, Love, Health and Success

Inspiration for a Woman's Soul: Opening to Gratitude & Grace

Inspiration for a Woman's Soul: Cultivating Joy

Inspiration for a Woman's Soul: Choosing Happiness

Embracing Your Authentic Self: Women's Stories of Self-Discovery & Transformation

Juicy, Joyful Life: Inspiration from Women Who Have Found the Sweetness in Every Day

Unleash Your Inner Magnificence (ebook only)

The Wisdom of Midlife Women 2 (ebook only)

You can find the majority of the titles at major online retailers and at bookstores by request.

The empowering stories in *Reclaiming Your Midlife Mojo* will inspire women to say "yes" to living their boldest dreams–no matter their age. Each empowering story will encourage readers to release their old patterns and embrace the powerful woman within. I recommend this book wholeheartedly to every woman who is ready to honor her inner wisdom and consciously create the life she desires.

CHRISTY WHITMAN

Transformational Leader, Messenger for The Council of Light and New York Times *bestselling author of* The Art of Having It All

The stories within *Reclaiming Your Midlife Mojo* are powerful testimonies to the strength and resilience of a woman's spirit. Their heartfelt and courageous stories will inspire you to make the invincible and empowered choices in your life.

AMY LEIGH MERCREE

Medical Intuitive and bestselling author of sixteen books including The Healing Home: A Room-by-Room Guide to Positive Vibes *and* A Little Bit of Goddess

Linda Joy has done it again with *Reclaiming Your Midlife Mojo*! This book is for every woman who has ever questioned herself and gone on to reclaim her inner light, unique magic, and feminine wisdom. You will be inspired to be the best version of YOU when you read the stories of these remarkable women.

LISA MANYON

The Business Marketing Architect, president of Write On Creative and author of Spiritual Sugar

The greatest gift in life is finding your authentic self. The powerful stories in *Reclaiming Your Midlife Mojo* will inspire you to think about the path you are on and open you to new possibilities in your life. Linda's books never disappoint.

NANCY OKEEFE

Human Design specialist

Touching, clear, inspiring, uplifting, and illuminating. As always, any book project that is produced by Linda Joy creates a massive ripple effect of positive impact and *Reclaiming Your Midlife Mojo* is no exception. The contributors' depth of self-inquiry and willingness to vulnerably share will leave the reader with a treasure trove of affirmation for their own journey along with a light on the path that radiates hope, joy, and possibility. No matter what the challenges the midlife passage contains, this book is the ready companion that will get you through it.

ANJEL B. HARTWELL

Wealthy Life Mentor and five-time award winning podcast host of Wickedly Smart Women Podcast

Midlife is a huge transitional point in a woman's journey. Life catches up to you, you're faced with the past challenges and the choices that have you brought you to this moment. You can stay the same or step through the buried blocks and fears that are keeping you from the joy you are meant to have. The amazing authors in *Reclaiming Your Midlife Mojo* share their courageous and intimate stories of facing fear, making hard choices, and persevering through the unimaginable. Each story brings an invaluable lesson of heartfelt wisdom and unmeasured strength to the reader.

MAL DUANE

Crystal chakra energy healer

Reclaiming Your Midlife Mojo is a potent compilation of stories that will inspire you to open your heart to what is possible in midlife! If you are feeling stagnant or find yourself at a midlife crossroads, you will be energized by each author's willingness to shake things up and commit to all that is possible when you embrace the magic of maturity!

SHANN VANDER LEEK

Podcast coach and bestselling author

All women have an innate wisdom that when shared, has the power to inspire, empower and support other women on their soul's path. The transformational stories shared in *Reclaiming Your Midlife Mojo* will awaken you to embrace your courageous heart, tap into the wisdom of your soul and take brave action to cocreate the divine life you envision.

DR. DEBRA L. REBLE

Intuitive psychologist, transformational life coach, women's retreat leader, and international best-selling author

There is nothing more inspiring for a woman than when a group of empowered women share the courage and perseverance they encountered when changing course midlife. Each story is insightful of just how powerful we can be as women. Life presents us all with challenges, but it is up to us to answer the heart's call to the magic within.

KIMMBERLY WOTIPKA

Spiritual advisor and Sacred Possibilities mentor

Foreword

DR. ELLEN ALBERTSON, THE MIDLIFE WHISPERER™

*A*re you longing for change? Want to get unstuck and find the confidence, energy, and clarity to transform yourself? Have you lost your magic and want it back? Would you like to wake up joyful, vibrant, and excited to start your day?

You're not alone. Many, if not most, midlife women feel this way.

Midlife is challenging and stressful. As Brené Brown says, "Midlife is not a crisis. Midlife is an unraveling." In fact, there is a U-shaped happiness curve that shows that on average life satisfaction hits a low point at midlife. The good news is, you can make the most of your upswing by discovering and transforming yourself. And the Universe is ready, willing, and able to support your heart's desire and call to own your light.

Transformation is many things: challenging, glorious, and scary. Like a caterpillar becoming a butterfly, the work entails weaving a chrysalis, digesting old parts of yourself, and breaking free so you can fly. In the process you become the heroine of your own journey and rediscover your magic.

In my life and work coaching hundreds of midlife women through physical, mental, emotional, spiritual, and relationship challenges, I have discovered that midlife metamorphosis happens in two ways: you consciously decide to shift, or the Universe steps in and triggers a transformation. Both scenarios require you to face fear, deal with discomfort, and be vulnerable.

During this confusing process the ego meltdowns, and the alchemy begins. As you confront your shadows–the people pleaser, inner critic, perfectionist, workaholic...and allow the Universe to vacuum up the masks and cobwebs blocking your light you break wide open and shine.

What's fascinating about the process is that like all Lepidoptera (the insect order comprising butterflies and moths), your DNA–your essence or soul cells–remain the same. Yet there's an inner shift that leads to a new, more authentic you. You feel, and may even look, different, and your world, energy, and what you attract also transform.

As I've written about in my book, *Rock Your Midlife: 7 Steps to Transform Yourself and Make Your Next Chapter Your Best Chapter,* I have experienced and witnessed both self-generated and Universe generated transformations. Sensing an inner restlessness, my own midlife whisperer has encouraged me to switch careers, go back to school, and leave a twenty-five-year marriage. And the Universe... well, she's has hit me up with numerous health chal-lenges–Hashimoto's Disease (an autoimmune disorder that destroys the thyroid gland), blindness (my retina detached three times), and most recently breast cancer. She's also blessed me with a new love and life that's life better than I imagined.

What's my superpower? Self-compassion, treating yourself like a good friend especially in those dark moments where you can barely get out of bed let alone take your next step. I highly recommend making it yours too. Why? It's a parachute allowing you to rise and take risks and a life vest enabling you to stay afloat when the waves of change knock you down. Plus, practicing self-compassion increases self-love, which is like pixie dust.

In this powerful book, Linda Joy has gathered a kaleidoscope of butterflies, a band of empowered women who have faced darkness and self-doubt, done their transformational work, and reclaimed their midlife mojo. Some no longer able to ignore their inner whispers, shouts, or yearnings made a conscious, intentional decision to change. Others faced a crucible crisis, Humpty Dumpty moments–like cancer or COVID 19–when life fell apart and they were forced to dig deep, go on a journey of self-discovery, and transform.

Looking for a sign that it's time to let go of the old you and discover your authentic self? Consider this book your wake-up call. Taking time to read these chapters is your first step to make your next chapter your best chapter. Within its pages you will find the inspiration, wisdom, and guidance you need to succeed. The stories within will empower you and help you realize that everything you require for your journey–courage, clarity, compassion, resilience–is already within you. You will learn that it's okay and even normal to be terrified, make mistakes, fail, and not know the way or how because life is a spiral not a straight line. The goal is to get comfortable with discomfort, turn challenges into opportunities, see solutions rather than problems, and enjoy not dread the journey.

Whether you want to transform your health or relationships, find your life purpose, and/or elevate your self-worth, this book will motivate you to get moving. When life calls you to reclaim your mojo, rather than hiding under the covers with Netflix and a bag of chips you will listen to your inner wisdom, show up, and rise.

The recipe to reclaim your inner mojo is simple–equal parts authenticity and courage, a cup of self-love, a large dash of vitality, and a tablespoon of progress (not perfection). Sprinkle with intention and bake in the oven of co-creation until cooked. All you must do is take that first step - whether big or small. Say "yes" to yourself and no to all the people, places, and things (including the inner voice of fear and doubt) that are keeping you stuck in reverse.

Remember, you are stronger and more important and powerful than you realize. As a midlife woman, you influence up to four generations–grandchildren, children, peers, and elders. You incarnated for a reason: to grow, glow, and make a difference.

My prayer is that you will take that first step because you are here to come alive and make a difference. Plus, when you shine you give other midlife women permission to do the same. In the words of the Dali Lama, "The world will be saved by the western women." The world is rapidly transforming and needs your light, love, and magic.

May you be safe, may you be happy, may you be healthy, may you reclaim your mojo.

Namaste,

Dr. Ellen Albertson
The Midlife Whisperer™
www.TheMidlifeWhisperer.com

Table of Contents

Introduction

LINDA JOY, PUBLISHER

"People may call what happens at midlife 'a crisis,' but it's not. It's an unraveling–a time when you feel a desperate pull to live the life you want to live, not the one you're 'supposed' to live. The unraveling is a time when you are challenged by the universe to let go of who you think you are supposed to be and to embrace who you are."

Brené Brown

*U*nraveling.

Take that in for a moment.

The line in Brené Brown's quote, "It's an unraveling–a time when you feel a desperate pull to live the life you want to live, not the one you're 'supposed' to live," has always resonated with me on a deep level because it captures the essence of my experiences over the last thirty years.

Over time, I've learned to trust my 'unravelings' as guidance from my wise inner self, soul whispers that rose, nudging me that it was time to shed yet another layer of beliefs, stories, and patterns that did not align with the highest truth of who I am–or of who I am becoming.

At sixty years old, I've leaned into this discomfort time and time again and discovered that the more I honored my truth and not the *shoulds* and *have-tos* I had been living, fulfillment, deeper inner peace, and joy awaited on the other side.

There comes a time in every woman's midlife journey, whether at thirty-five or sixty, when she experiences a yearning from within–a restlessness, a calling–from the deepest recesses of her heart beckoning her to own her light.

For sixteen years, as publisher of *Aspire Magazine* and as an Intentional Living Guide™ and Mindset Mojo™ Mentor, I've been in sacred community with women worldwide. Whether sitting around the kitchen table with girlfriends or in a virtual community with my audience of women on the path of self-discovery, I have witnessed a richness and an emotional depth to the conversations.

I listen deeply to the language my clients and audience use, and I've noticed a shift in the words being used to describe their experiences–especially over the last three years:

Unfolding, awakening, becoming, honoring, rising, shedding.

These are just some words that women have used to describe their midlife transformation and the inner awakening they are experiencing.

A shift is happening. Maybe you're feeling the call too, my beautiful friend.

Maybe you're experiencing the call as a yearning that shows up as a gentle nudge whispering to you. Maybe it manifests as a shout with a sense of urgency–calling you to own your truth and light.

No matter how it shows up, it's a calling to reclaim your inner mojo–your unique magic and feminine wisdom.

I know those soul whispers well.

They have been guiding me along my life's path for decades. As the back cover of this book shares:

As a woman says "yes" to her inner light, she sheds the illusions of who she thought she had to be, the roles she thought she had to play, and the limiting beliefs about her self-worth to discover that within her was the magic to co-create her life from a place of truth and authenticity.

On that day, she will come face-to-face with her inner mojo–her divine essence–and the two will become one, embracing, dancing, and celebrating the home-coming.

Now is the time to say "yes" and come home to yourself, my beautiful friend.

The world needs your light. Within the pages of *Reclaiming Your Midlife Mojo,* you'll meet a collective of empowered women whose stories of self-discovery and transformation reflect the trust, resilience, and courage, it took to change course in the middle of their lives. You may even see yourself in one or more of the stories.

With vulnerable hearts, these authors share their stories to inspire you to say "yes" to your deepest calling and to reclaim your midlife mojo. Allow the journaling prompts shared at the end of each story to bring you deeper into your truth and support you in unraveling, and releasing, what no longer serves you.

May you find the inspiration and courage to follow the whispers of your soul and the calling of your heart and to embrace your midlife mojo.

Live an Intentional Life,

Linda Joy
Publisher

PART ONE
Health

Writing a New Chapter of Health and Wellness in Midlife

DR. COLLEEN GEORGES

I'd always referred to myself as a physically lazy person. I remember at my high school graduation when everyone around me was sad about leaving high school, I experienced joy because I'd never have to take gym class again. And in college, I recall wishing there was a golf cart I could just ride around in to get to my classes instead of having to walk around campus. I never liked sports, I never liked the gym, and whenever I saw someone post on social media about how running was their happy place, I'd think, *how on earth could running make you happy?* All that exertion just seemed awful.

And healthy eating? Forget that. I liked my glass of red wine each night, and my pint of Haagen-Dazs. Don't get me wrong, I *tried* to get my eating act together a gazillion times. But honestly, it was never about getting healthy, it was always about losing weight. When I was in my twenties and thirties, I did your typical crash diets. I'd count my calories, tell myself diet soda and black coffee were healthy because they had zero calories, and make sure I left room for wine. Once I lost weight, I quickly fell back into my usual *unhealthier* habits. That was my pattern for years.

I started 2020 working with a wonderful health coach and I developed some healthier habits. But then, COVID hit. Like most folks, my anxiety spiked. I knew I needed to be mentally and emotionally present for my coaching clients, so, I gave myself a coping mechanism—food and wine. It was a poor decision, and I knew it, but I made it anyway. And, throughout 2020, I fed, and drank, my fears. I ate whatever I felt like whenever I felt like it. And each night at eight p.m., I'd pour myself a progressively larger glass of red wine. I literally went to the store and bought a larger glass so it could fit more wine. I ordered boxes of wine and got them delivered to my house. With time, I'd begun thinking about my nightly glass of wine earlier and earlier in the day, wanting eight p.m. to come faster. I convinced myself the wine helped me sleep and was good for me by warding off heart disease and stuff like that. But underneath it all, there was a truth I knew—I was craving it and relying on it, and that seemed super adjacent to addiction.

There's only so long you can hide from yourself. I knew I was making destructive decisions.

Throughout 2020, all of us witnessed people of all ages get horribly sick and die from COVID. In my mid-forties, I found myself fully realizing that life was really fragile. By the end of 2020, it hit me that I had to treat my body better. I treated it like garbage instead of with respect. I suddenly recognized that everything I did to or did for, my body, now was going to determine what my body could do for me, ten, twenty, thirty years from then. I had to stop abusing it. I finally wanted to make my health and well-being a priority. It wasn't too late. I could begin immediately.

On January 8, 2021, I gave up drinking alcohol. What a journey. My body had forgotten how to sleep without it. I was waking up an average of four times a night. I tried various supplements at the health food store and replacing the wine with tea and other healthier drinks before bed. After a few months of sleep issues (aka withdrawal), my body adjusted, and I slept beautifully. As I write this, I'm over a year alcohol free.

As a result of my eating vices in 2020 (and quite frankly, before 2020), I'd gained quite a bit of weight and felt lethargic and physically uncomfortable. I wanted to make a change, but I knew I couldn't make it all about weight loss, it had to be about long-term health and well-being. I'd need to learn how to eat mindfully and intentionally and to teach myself about nutrition, so I could sustain any positive outcomes I achieved, including, hopefully, long-term health. I started using a food tracking app to begin eating with intention while creating accountability for myself. I took some courses in health and nutrition, and I learned. I read about protein. I made water and vegetables my friends. I mainly just drink water, tea, and unsweetened iced tea, as I gave up soda in 2018 and coffee in 2019. I taught myself about red and green superfoods and supplements. I created eating routines and paid attention to my hunger so I could avoid mindless eating. I'm proud to say that I've been eating mindfully and intentionally for over a year now and I feel full of energy and focus like never before in my life.

Then, I decided to take my mindful and intentional eating to another level. As an animal lover, I'd always had cognitive dissonance about eating meat and fish. I mean, I don't even kill bugs. I get upset when I realize I've accidentally stepped on a bug. So, being a carnivore never fit my beliefs or values. I tried to eat vegetarian a few times throughout my twenties, thirties, and forties. I never

9

made it very long though. I'd eventually crave a pork roll, an egg and cheese sandwich, or chicken parmesan, and I'd give into my craving and be done with it. Having sustained positive eating habits through 2021, in August, I decided to give it a go again, feeling like I was genuinely ready to give up meat and fish this time. Quickly into this journey, I decided to take it to the next level and go vegan, letting go of dairy and eggs altogether. It's been over eight months now and I can say that it's not nearly as hard as I expected. I've found many awesome meat substitutes, fabulous vegetable and plant-based meals, and great vegan snacks. I've also found that most restaurants have vegan options.

Now, about that physically lazy person thing–it was beyond time I stopped telling myself that story. The only form of exercise I'd ever liked was walking. However, when I walked, it had never been in an effort to exercise, it was because I absolutely love nature. I can get lost in trees, flowers, grass, sky, wind, and animals. Making walking my major form of exercise was worth a shot. So, on January 22, 2021, I started taking a walk a day. Immediately, I noticed a boost in my sense of peace and joy. This made the physical aspect of it much easier. I quickly became hooked. While I've missed a day here and there, I've taken at least a thirty-minute walk nearly daily for over a year. I joke that walking is totally my new wine–I think about it as soon as I wake up, I crave it, and I rely on it for my overall wellbeing. It has also led me to explore numerous local gardens, parks, and hiking trails that have brought me immense joy and opportunities for connection with the people I love.

But I also knew I wanted exercise to become a part of my morning routine. I'd never really had a morning routine but had always kind of wished I did. I wondered, perhaps the treadmill with an audiobook might be a nice way to start my day? I'd tried the treadmill thing before. I even kept it up for two months once. But alas, I wasn't consistent and always stopped. However, I knew I wanted to start my day by getting my blood, brain, and energy flowing, and the treadmill seemed like a good way to do that. Fifteen minutes first thing each morning after I brushed my teeth, washed my face, put in my contacts, fed the cats, and packed my son's school lunch. That was it. I've barely missed a day since I began on February 2, 2021. Using the treadmill started my day with positive energy and motivation. Plus, I got a ton of ideas and inspiration from the audiobooks I listened to during my treadmill time.

The eradication of alcohol, the addition of mindful eating, and the daily walking culminated in me losing forty-five pounds. I'm proud of this outcome, but even prouder that I maintained the habits that helped me achieve it because they have become more valuable to me than the loss of weight itself. These physical health habits have transformed my life and my well-being completely, including my mental and emotional wellness. I feel more energetic, focused, motivated, joyful, and peaceful. I decided to stop telling myself a story about my health shortcomings and rescript myself a story of sustainable wellness. It's never too late to change your narrative.

Reflection

Where does cognitive dissonance show up in your life and how do you intentionally address it?

What habits do you have that no longer serve you, and what new habits can you replace them with? Which habit will you focus on first?

In what ways has making an intention change in your life resulted in positive unintended outcomes? How have these changes impacted your life?

The Beauty of Humble Surrender

LISA HROMADA

*T*he day had grown dark by the time they wheeled me into the surgery room. I vividly recall the cold and uncomfortable feeling of the hospital bed. How could I forget? I'd been laying on it for more than four hours, covered only in a thin hospital gown and a semi-stiff blanket, waiting for my procedure to start. A procedure that I never expected to experience for a second time–the end of another lovingly planned pregnancy.

I couldn't help but think of my two-year-old son back home. It was the first time since his birth that he would not be able to snuggle next to me as he went to sleep. Anxiousness, guilt, and a longing to be home washed over me as I imagined him wondering where mommy was, why she was not with him, and when she would be home.

My husband and I always knew that we wanted to have children. In fact, I knew my entire life that I was meant to be a mom. Many times, I envisioned what it would be like to be pregnant, how I would share the news, and the experience of bringing a new life into the world. It never occurred to me that I would experience three losses.

13

The Beauty of Humble Surrender

We were in our early thirties when we were ready to start a family. A few months into trying, I was ecstatic to discover I was pregnant. I never considered that anything could or would go wrong, especially after seeing a heartbeat at our eight-week ultrasound. But, to our shock and devastation, at twelve weeks we were told that there was no longer a heartbeat, and I would need to have a D&C procedure.

I felt gutted–both from the grief in my heart and the emptiness in my womb. I was spiritually lost, alone, and angry. Thoughts like, "It wasn't supposed to happen to *me*," played in my mind. For months, I rarely slept. My husband would wake in the middle of the night to find me crying and journaling. I was lost in the grief, unaware of how to make my way out.

Three months later, I was relieved to discover I was again pregnant. The grief from my first loss began to dissolve, until my eight-week ultrasound when we discovered there was no heartbeat. "Why!?" I desperately asked God. I spent the following months secretly obsessing over getting pregnant again. It consumed my thoughts. Although I was good at hiding my anguish from the outside world, inside I was deeply suffering. I knew I needed a change. After months of obsessive thoughts and emotional suffering, I felt an inner nudge to release control over this part of my life and allow a Divine plan to flow through.

Within a few months of making this choice, I discovered I was pregnant with our son–a most precious gift after an agonizing journey. I recall the moment he was placed on my chest immediately after his birth. He looked up at me with tear-filled eyes, and I felt the deepest sense of love, connection, and gratitude.

Two years after the joyful arrival of our son, we were excited to discover I was again pregnant. Everything was going smoothly until I was just over three months along.

I was out of state visiting family with our son, excited to share our pregnancy news, when I got a call from my doctor's office. Reality quickly sunk in that this would be my third loss, and a second time requiring a procedure. I began to sob, feeling defeated, and unsure of how to tell my husband.

The following two weeks awaiting my procedure were filled with shame, guilt, profound sadness, and a desperate reaching for answers and peace. I'd lost a part of myself, and I knew I needed a fresh start beyond my grief. I needed Divine help–a Divine reset–where I could release my suffering and enjoy my many blessings.

With nowhere else to go for peace and answers, I went in prayerful surrender and tearful conversation with God. In so many words, I said, "I give myself and my life to you. If you have a purpose for me, please reveal it to me differently. You know what is in my heart (and I declared what my desired life looked like), and I give myself and my life to your purpose." I came to a point where no matter what the future held, I wanted my days to be filled with inner peace, joy, purpose, and fulfillment. I was going to do what I could to help make that happen; the rest I placed in Divine hands.

There's something beautiful about humble surrender. It is the understanding that nothing is solely my doing, but a consistent co-creative effort of love and purpose. When I surrendered, I shed a part of my ego that was holding onto my "problems." Instead, I focused on how *good* could manifest through me. It's a completely different energy to live in–a sacred, peaceful, and divine energy of solutions. I made a plan that I would set into motion after my procedure.

So, there I was back in the surgery room looking up at the sterile white walls and bright ceiling lights feeling more vulnerable and exposed than I ever have in my life.

The Beauty of Humble Surrender

I listened to the humming of the machines as a team of nurses strapped my legs apart and secured my arms to my sides. Despite their attempts to keep me warm, I could still feel the icy air in the room wash over my skin.

Although I was now in a place of acceptance about my circumstances, my thirty-six-year-old body still wept. After all, for the past fifteen weeks, it lovingly held more than a developing new life; it held special hopes, dreams, and plans for our growing family. Just before submitting to the anesthesia, I could feel one tear stream down my cheek. Perhaps it was my body's way of saying its final goodbye to the life it once held.

Upon waking, with my eyes still closed, I could see a bright white light. It wasn't the light from the room; it carried an energy of love, hope, and a sacred guiding presence. I smiled with a knowing that my path was about to change. Although the following months were not without the occasional feelings of emptiness and grief, my perspective, and the way I chose to live my life had shifted.

I came to the profound realization that challenges will never cease to exist in my life, but if I can find ways of navigating these times through the lens of gratitude, awareness, and an empowered life view, then I'll always be making the best of the days I'm blessed with. I chose to no longer be hindered by fear, doubt, and self-defeating thoughts, or bound by my past or tied to a specific future. I felt inspired to create empowering practices to support me in finding my way back to joy and inner peace whenever limiting thoughts and hindering emotions arose. I discovered, and now teach, the importance of focusing on the things, people, and thoughts that help lead us there.

Fast forward a half year after having that conversation with God, I awoke one morning from a vivid dream where I was shown a positive pregnancy test that read, "healthy pregnancy." Nine months later, our beautiful, healthy daughter was born—a true light of joy and a reminder that grace flows freely when we trust, love, and surrender.

I realize now that although considerably challenging at times, this was a journey that had to be taken so that I may awaken more fully to my higher path and a higher purpose. It is a journey that has led me to enjoying two precious children and stronger relationships. It is a journey that gave me a fulfilling, spirit-led business empowering women to embrace a sacred solutions-centered lifestyle, so they too can co-create a life that brings inner peace, joy, and self-acceptance. I continue to experience the truth that life is not about arriving at a specific destination, but it's about how I navigate and enjoy the journey to get there. This is where lasting joy, peace, and satisfaction reside. This is how I continue to live an empowered life.

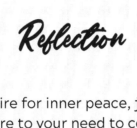

Reflection

Describe your desire for inner peace, joy, and happiness bigger and compare to your need to control how it manifests.

How are you willing to take intentional action where you can and release the rest to your Source to help guide you to your highest potential?

What are you willing to do to make an empowered choice each day to no longer be hindered by fear, doubt, and self-defeating thoughts and limiting beliefs so you can embrace an empowered life?

Thriving Through the Big C

VERA VENTURA

*Y*ou have cancer in both breasts," the doctor said.

Excuse me? Me? Are you sure? I thought, *WHAT? That makes no sense! I don't drink. I don't smoke. I am a yoga teacher. I have been in recovery for seventeen years. I meditate daily. Clearly, you have the wrong lady!*

I learned that in this case, it didn't matter. I was dealt a bad hand of genetics inherited from my father. I didn't inherit much from my father except for a few dusty books and well, cancer. Thanks, Dad!

The cancer journey is akin to reading a book and writing a narrative at the same time. There's a prescribed way of doing things, provided by your doctors and the institutions that specialize in cancer support, but there's also the internal compass that guides you along the path. That internal compass might lead you in other directions in order to seek alternative approaches and experiences. In turn, you end up writing your story, one that can't be found in a doctor's manual.

Upon receiving the diagnosis, I felt a flood of emotions such as disbelief, anger, sadness, and fear. At thirty-nine, I had two small children, and a husband working on a film in Saudi Arabia. A transplant after college, I lived in Boston, where I got healthy and sane, but had no familial roots.

At the age of fourteen, I left home in Miami to live with my sister in New York City.

I relied on substances and partying to provide the escapism I craved. So, while high school students were studying for tests and involved in extra-curricular clubs, the only clubs that I frequented were those with a DJ and an open bar.

By the time I graduated college, I felt broken. Whatever spark that initially emanated from the light of youth had been extinguished in a constant need to escape from pain. A prisoner of my mind's negative thinking, I compared myself to everyone, and the majority of the time I didn't measure up. I suffered from an eating disorder and an insatiable appetite to constantly fill an internal emptiness. The substance didn't matter as long as I could escape my feelings.

Everything came crashing to a halt when I hit an emotional and spiritual bottom. But as the saying goes, it's because of the crack that the light can enter. For me, the light entered in the form of a twelve-step program specifically designed to help with eating disorders.

What I learned was that the eating disorder was part of a greater picture of addiction. I used substances to numb my feelings. Food was my first drug of choice and then the addiction evolved into many different forms, like a monster with several heads. When I finally put down the substances, I began to feel the feelings.

And boy was that not easy. While it was one of the hardest things I've done, I couldn't deny the gifts that came from doing the work. I developed a connection to a power greater than myself. Some call it God, Higher Power, Allah, Yahweh, Universe, The Source, Mother, etc.

What you call it doesn't really matter just as long as you are not at the center of it all.

Miracle of miracles! I was able to partake in social situations and feel uncomfortable without running and getting high! I could just feel the feelings, without going into a dark pit of negative thinking, fear, and despair. I could meditate, sit quietly, and control my negative thinking. I discovered that the resentments and fears I carried from my past did not need to own and dictate the outcome of my future.

When I was diagnosed with cancer, I was able to "cash in" the healthy deposits made over the years to my spiritual piggy bank. I deepened my connection to my higher power. Sure, I would have a good cry, but in order to stay out of the negativity and future tripping, I got into action by calling a friend, going to a yoga class, or doing service for someone in need. In other words, getting out of my head and getting into my soul.

I didn't want to fight cancer, I wanted to learn from it. I wanted it to teach me, I wanted to grow with it. I spent hours in the hospital learning about my diagnosis and inherited genetics. I learned what foods best supported prevention and what natural therapies complimented the Western approach.

And I shared my findings and knowledge every step of the way, because it helped. Imbuing the sharing with lightness and positivity made the journey easier. For instance, while receiving the intense blood colored chemotherapy "Red Devil" aka Adriamycin and Cytoxan, I made a video explaining how the drugs were administered and how to combat some of the side effects such as nausea, vomiting, and constipation.

Through the treatment, I never stopped my yoga and teaching practice. I taught holistic health classes from my hospital bed! Sure, I took pauses, but staying active made

21

me happier. The connection was evident. Here I was writing my own narrative.

Some people were genuinely concerned that I was doing too much and not taking it seriously. An interesting dilemma on the cancer path, other people's fears being projected on you! Thus, it was incredibly important to keep in fit spiritual connection. I knew my truth along the way–despite the "noise" of others. When I got quiet in meditation, I received tremendous insight. I created a spiritual fortress, even in the hospital. I carried my crystals, diffuser, oils, warm blankets, and calming music everywhere I went. I embedded the experience with positive light and energy despite the circumstances.

Just had a double mastectomy? No problem. Sniff some lavender and enjoy the warm broth given to you right after you wake up from anesthesia. Every moment can be magical. It's a choice. This mindset carried me through breast cancer, and what I wasn't fully prepared for was when breast cancer metastasized to my brain.

After recovery from breast reconstruction, I went back to teaching yoga and I started having shooting pains that traveled from the base of my spine up to the top of my head. It got so bad I had to stop teaching. I also had trouble walking and running. Overall, my balance was off. Initially, I suspected a pinched nerve and consulted a chiropractor and acupuncturist. I got temporary relief, but then fell back into pain.

Finally, I couldn't eat or move. My husband rushed me to the emergency room whereby it was discovered I had a tumor, the size of an organic strawberry, lodged into my brain.

Following the hero's journey outline, this is the point of the story that the hero gets eaten by the dragon. Where the hero says, "I think I am a goner." But because of the spiritual fortress I had built, I kept calm, open, and grounded. Dare I even say, grateful!

Finally, I learned what was causing pain all these months and was no longer in the dark, pondering how I could live another day. "Kids, mom is sick because she had a tumor lodged in her cerebellum!"

Again, when you are most broken, that is when the light can enter. I felt if I were to die, at least I lived my life with integrity, honesty, and openness. I learned to love fully and release my ego.

But, of course, I didn't want to die.

Whisked away into a world of medical interventions, brilliant doctors, and cutting-edge technology, I remained in awe of the efficiency and the ability to open up a brain and remove a tumor. Sure, I had a brain tumor, but damn I was lucky to be living in this day and age! Now I have a reconstructed body and a vacant space in the back of my head. I feel like the Bionic Woman.

I am not a breast cancer warrior. I did not slay or fuck anything along my journey. Rather, I moved through it gracefully, fluidly, and connected with a source of light along the way. That light came from inner wisdom and trust that could only be understood when there's silence. That's how I became the Breast Cancer Goddess.

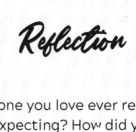

Reflection

Have you or someone you love ever received a diagnosis that you weren't expecting? How did you handle the news? What would you do differently?

What parts of your story do you hide from others due to feelings of shame or lack? What would change if you shared your experiences from a healed place?

We often use the terms "survivor" or "warrior" to describe women who have lived through cancer. How do these terms sit with you, or not? In what ways does our language impact our experiences—and what descriptors have you adopted that may not serve you?

My Body Kept Score

KAREN SHIER

*O*n a cold and dreary January morning, my new husband and I boarded a plane in Detroit heading for Fort Myers, Florida, to celebrate my fiftieth birthday and spend a week of fun in the sun. After a grueling year of his international travel and my endless hours of work as a corporate vice president of Human Resources, we needed this getaway.

As I disembarked from the plane, I felt the warm, moist, salty Florida air on my skin. I breathed it in, feeling a warm rush of happiness. We grabbed our rental car and drove to the beautiful hotel that would be our home for the week.

I opened the door to the hotel room and discovered my husband had pre-arranged a beautiful bouquet of roses and a bottle of wine. What a lovely way to celebrate a milestone–the culmination of the half-century I'd been alive.

Wine in hand, we stepped out onto our balcony to view the beautiful waterways, sand, and trees surrounding the hotel, not to mention the ocean. We were excited about the whole week we had ahead of us.

25

My husband put his hand on my waist, drew me close, and whispered in my ear, "Happy birthday, honey," clinking my glass in a toast.

We set off on our island adventures the next morning, driving along the Intercoastal Waterway, windows down, reveling in the feel of the sun on our skin. We enjoyed watching manatees, sunsets over the ocean, and lovely walks among brightly colored homes throughout the week.

On the day before our return home, we discovered that our hotel had a private island. We both needed to relax, and dreading our flight back to the snow, donned our swimsuits and headed out.

On the ferry trip to the tiny island sandbar, we were flanked by beautiful dolphins escorting us to the destination. Upon arrival, we walked along the shore amongst the other sunbathers, looking for shells, wading out into the beautiful cool waters, and allowing our lily-white skin to soak up the beautiful warm rays of sunshine. In those three hours, we had no cares in the world. Well, almost none.

That day on the sandbar, I saw beautiful, tanned bodies enjoying their lovely sunbathing routine. As I sat there holding back tears, I thought *there just had to be more to life. Why was my life consistently so hard? Why didn't I love the job I worked so hard at and dedicated my life to? Why was I constantly feeling that life had been sucked out of me?*

I reflected through my tears that I had not been feeling well for some time. I couldn't seem to keep my blood pressure under control. I had difficulty walking any distance without feeling weak, breathless, and fatigued. I felt this nagging sense of sadness and depression, of hopelessness, and powerlessness about my job and the feeling I couldn't escape it. I was stuck.

Since my early twenties, I had struggled with my weight. I had endured heartbreaks, losing three babies to stillbirth and miscarriage, and gratefully accomplished one successful pregnancy after six months of bed rest. Then, my dad passed away suddenly at fifty-seven, plunging me into estate responsibilities. My first marriage of seventeen years ended; I became a single mom for ten years, which added another layer of responsibility.

Additionally, my pursuit of education and certifications required studies in every free moment of my adult life. In 2008, when the U.S. economy was in shambles, twenty years of retirement savings were lost, child support stopped coming in, and my employer-issued sizeable pay cuts to the management team. I had clung to the corporate ladder for two decades. Chronic stress was abundant. Me time was non-existent.

Hard work was all I had ever known. I had beliefs and imprints about what was expected of me and how to achieve success. My sense of responsibility had me putting my needs behind others. My health was in serious trouble, and I was an emotional mess. That day on the beach, I decided it was time to overcome my fears and plan for my job to end.

Unfortunately, freedom from the job took more time than anticipated.

Eighteen months after the vacation, while undergoing numerous tests for the heart attack-like pain that came with no warning, it was determined that my gall bladder had become diseased and needed to come out. I had high hopes for relief for about six weeks then the pain started again. *Crap!*

Then the compliance part of my job became more stressful. New laws seemingly appeared daily. My staff and I were buried in work and often the last to leave the office.

27

I was overworked, underappreciated, and shockingly unhealthy for my age. The chest pains, which felt like someone was taking the sharp end of a Campbell's soup lid and twisting it through my sternum to my back, became more intense and frequent. These attacks came at any moment, lasted hours, and left me weak and fearful of the next occurrence.

Another year of tests passed by, and I learned I had a hiatal hernia large enough to require another surgery with a long recovery. My stomach, full of ulcers from years of chronic stress, had moved up through my diaphragm into my chest cavity, a condition that could prove instantly fatal. Additionally, my body had developed a precancerous condition called Barrett's Esophagus. Let's just add those tidbits to the worry—oh my!

While waiting for the subsequent surgery, the pain became unbearable. I struggled to eat solid foods, and my liquid diet was far from satisfying. Some days, I wanted to just go to sleep and not wake up. I felt my body was dying. My exhaustion and poor health continued, and I grew to hate my unfulfilling compliance job, sometimes crying in the car on my way to work. Finally, I heard myself saying out loud, "I do not want to die at my desk!"

I was an absolute mess! The gift from this struggle became my wake-up call. My body finally convinced me that the path I was on was not working. I knew it was life or death for me, and immediate action was needed. I was now forced to deal with my fears of leaving my job.

I sought advice. My new husband loved, supported, and believed in me unconditionally. A psychologist helped me work through my many fears about leaving my job. My life coach helped me see there was a life beyond my job. They all put it to me this way, "What is this job costing you?"

It didn't take me long to figure out, "Well, EVERYTHING!"

What did I want to do with the second half of my life?

I knew I wanted to write and help women understand the importance of self-care. I knew I could utilize my experiences to lead in an enlightened and empowered way. Coaching was where my heart was calling!

I took inspired actions. I started my healing journey while still at my job. I found the right coaching certification programs and surrounded myself with the spiritual women I wanted to emulate. I became an energy master. Life started feeling fun and exciting.

I worked to release old beliefs that no longer served me. I forgave myself for past actions and others for hurting me. Instead of wallowing in my old job story, I pivoted, set aside my anger, and became grateful for what my job had provided. I embraced my inner goddess. I took back my power. My life was meant to be joyful and didn't have to be hard like I had made it.

I spoke with my manager and strategically planned for my departure. I saved money to pay bills ahead. I developed a succession plan to put my staff into the right roles. Finally, I focused on securing the resources I needed to start my own business.

I waited for the right time to retire early, to leave my job gracefully, feeling good about it. Four years of focused planning, learning, and healing after that tearful day on the sandbar, and I made it happen at just the right time for me. I've released the weight, regained my health, become an author, and a coach; I work with amazing women, and I've never looked back!

Reflection

What have you experienced in your life that became a pivotal wake-up call for you?

Who has supported you unconditionally and without judgment, and how did their love make a difference for your life?

In what ways are you putting yourself first and in what ways are you finding yourself to be the last person served?

Experiencing Surrender

FELICIA MESSINA-D'HAITI

I could see the finish line so clearly. August 31, 2020, would be the five-year-anniversary of my stage three colon cancer diagnosis. I looked forward with great joy and excitement to the end of this period of colon cancer treatments, scans, and medical appointments. I was also looking forward to no longer being a frequent visitor to the medical center. One experience I never dreamed of having, was being recognized by all the medical personnel due to the frequency of my doctor visits. All of my check-ups with the oncologist had been going well, and I was healing and thriving. I was more than ready to close that chapter with gratitude for the lessons learned and I was ready to finally release those routines.

Typically, I schedule my annual physical exams in June after my birthday. That summer, the exams had been postponed due to pandemic restrictions. Everything checked out well with my physical, and then my doctor and I scheduled my mammogram before the end of August. It was at that mammogram that the discovery of "suspicious" cells overshadowed my joyful celebration. I felt defeated, even though this news was less shocking and less definite than when I was diagnosed with colon cancer. I had endured so much between the surgeries, chemotherapy, and recovery. I was still grieving the aspects of my life that I was forced to release. Yet, I finally felt my energy levels had improved, and that I was ready to move on. But here I was again, at the beginning of a new, and so far, unclear journey.

Over the next few months, I stepped back into frequent visitor status with the added layer of having to sit through each visit alone because only patients with appointments were allowed in the medical facilities. I also needed specialty scans using equipment that was not available at my usual medical facility, so I found myself navigating through unfamiliar emotional and physical territory. When I met with my oncologist at what should have been our final visit, he informed me that I now had another five years of monitoring though a final diagnosis had not been determined yet. After three months of CT scans, MRIs, and other diagnostic procedures, I became impatient with the process. The waiting between appointments was so frustrating. I convinced myself that it couldn't be that serious if the appointments were not considered emergencies, unlike the colon cancer diagnosis when my first surgery was scheduled within two weeks of detection.

While I waited in uncertainty, many of my thoughts focused on wondering what I hadn't learned from the first cancer experience, or what had I learned that I didn't follow through with. How was I responsible for this experience? Between the first and second experience, I had spent nearly half of the time in a personal discovery and development program. Had I not learned enough? Also, during this time, my only brother and my father transitioned. I felt angry, like here I was with another challenging time ahead. I felt tired from dealing with these challenges and unexpected experiences. I longed for a period of time where calm water prevailed.

Upon reflection, there were two lessons that stood out the most for me during those five years. One was in receiving support from others; knowing that I did not have to do it all myself. The other related to the importance of self-care on multiple levels. Not my previous simplistic view of self-care that involved participating in relaxing activities every once in a while, but a deeper acknowledgement of the type of self-care that is built into every aspect of my life, which governs the little daily decisions that I make. I had grown a great deal in these and many other areas; yet now, I felt as if I was being punished for not growing enough.

Not only did I feel a crushing sadness, but I was also overwhelmed by the complexity of the breast cancer diagnosis. Finally, after numerous scans, two surgeries and nearly five months later, I had a complete evaluation and diagnosis. The best news I received was that we caught it early, and the recommended treatment (after the last surgery) was twenty radiation treatments followed by five years of medication. Though I was extremely grateful that chemotherapy was not part of their recommended treatment, I was not pleased about having another five years of treatment and monitoring.

One early morning, as I sat in the dark heaviness of my feelings, I received an email from a friend. She wrote, "Are you up for a quick chat?" and I responded by giving her a call. She felt my sadness, and was concerned, so she urged me to step out of it before it swallowed me. Her questions opened my eyes to several patterns of thought in which I had become caught up. Her perspective provided me with another viewpoint from which to assess my current situation. After we finished that enlightening conversation, I felt as though a large portion of that dark

33

heaviness had been lifted from my heart space. After that one call, I became aware of how much I had participated in self-judgment. Every day, I was judging myself, asking questions, and making statements that granted me little grace. I felt like I should have known better. I had done so much personal development and spiritual work, why was this happening to me? So much had changed since my colon cancer diagnosis, yet it didn't seem to be enough. What else would I be asked to give up, to examine, or to change?

I will be forever grateful for these new awarenesses. That one conversation pulled me out of my experience and allowed me to look at my situation from another perspective. It snapped me out of the negative tornado of thoughts that I had created and was unconsciously feeding. At that point, I made a choice to shift my thoughts and create a more internally loving environment for myself. Even though I already knew much of what my friend had said, I had been so wrapped up in my own despair that I had not been ready to step out of it. Now, I was ready. So, what was next for me?

First, I recognized that I needed to forgive myself for all of the things I had been blaming myself for, including both the colon and the breast cancer diagnoses. Along with that, I also acknowledged that I had everything I needed—all the tools, knowledge, and experiences to re-direct my thoughts and beliefs, and to change the way I was treating myself. I began to re-engage in the morning and evening routines and spiritual practices that I had abandoned.

During this time and in the months following, while processing a wide range of emotions, a concept that emerged for me was that of surrender. I thought I had learned what I needed to about surrender during the previous five years of experiences until I realized that my definition of surrender had unspoken terms. I was agreeable with the concept of surrender as long as I felt like I had a degree of control in the matter. Now that I look back on that unconscious agreement, it doesn't even make sense to me. Yet, it was the root of much of my self-judgement and my non-acceptance of the circumstances.

Embracing and living the experience of surrender began a new and more joyful journey for me. Releasing the need to feel like I am in control of circumstances (that I was *never* in control of anyway) supports me in also releasing self-judgment, living in the present, and letting go of the fear of the unknown. Once I embraced the experience of surrender, I accepted my new cancer diagnosis as a neutral experience–one that I could choose how to view and journey through. Living my experiences through the lens of surrender allows for more grace, love, and joy.

Reflection

Are there opportunities for you to allow in others' support? How would your life be different if you accepted support when it was extended?

In what ways do you try to control situations? What might you release if you embraced surrender like Felicia did?

Where can you invite into your life a new perspective and less self-judgment? How would it feel in your body to do so?

My Way Didn't Work

CINDY WINSEL

*I*t all seemed like a horrible nightmare to me. At any moment, I expected to wake up with the morning sun struggling to peek through the blinds, just like so many mornings after a night of drinking. But my skin felt the horror and my eyes were not to be deceived. I was truly awake and among the AAers. All I could do was watch and listen until I could escape to the comfort of my bed.

The first time I went into recovery, I had no idea what recovery was, or why I was in an AA meeting. *I did not have a problem with alcohol,* I told myself I was drinking because my life was harder. At that time, I never told myself I would stop drinking. Drinking was my fun. Even still, I stopped drinking for three months.

Then I started drinking again and it became worse. Several of my colleagues pulled me aside and said I had lost the spark in my eyes, and they knew I was drinking again. At that point I went into recovery to please them and to get them off my back.

My therapist suggested I go to an AA meeting. It horrified me to think I would be sitting around a table

37

with a bunch of alcoholics. My idea of fun didn't include the smell of coffee in Styrofoam cups or saying my name and stating I was an alcoholic. The images shook me to my core. *Oh, hell no.*

I suppose my therapist got under my skin because I finally went to an AA meeting. I sat there quietly, hoping that no one would notice me. I attended a few more times, and they kept reminding me to find a sponsor. I thought if I ignored their suggestion, it would go away. One day a young woman came up to me after a meeting and asked if I needed a sponsor. Being the compliant one, I relented, and we began meeting. She insisted I call her daily, before noon, and check in. I could not leave a message or text. *Ugh, I hated this.* I did it for a while but at one point, I told her I thought it was pointless and unrealistic.

"I never talk to anyone daily," I said.

She calmly responded, "I will talk to you tomorrow. Have a wonderful day."

I knew I was heading toward a relapse before I relapsed. I was subconsciously, or maybe consciously, planning out my relapse. The first step was to text my sponsor and fire her. The second step was to stop going to AA meetings. I could not continue to do AA things and drink too, and I wanted to drink.

I picked up where I had left off. I figured I would do drinking my way. I attempted to only drink on the weekends and at night. Plus, I attempted to only drink at home, not when I was out with friends. Despite these attempts, my drinking became scary and dangerous for me and for others.

In the AA world, people often ask if you have hit your bottom. Have enough terrible things happened in your life that you are ready to get help for your drinking? I had so many bottoms, I lost count. I am surprised I still have a bottom. One morning I woke up with bruises all over one side of my body, and I had no memory of how I got them. It worried me for a minute, but I did not stop drinking. I made an ass out of myself on many occasions, and I kept drinking. I ended up in the hospital once due to my drinking but even that didn't stop me.

What stopped me? I am not certain it was this situation I am about to describe or if my Higher Power knocked me upside the head so many times, and this time I took notice. I still am not sure.

It was a beautiful fall day, and I had just come back from a run at a nearby park. In the middle of all this, I was training for a half marathon. I was at my boyfriend's house, and when I came back from my run, I rested on the couch for a while. It was late in the day, and like a good alcoholic, I figured it was a suitable time to have a glass of wine. My boyfriend poured us glasses of wine and later that evening we had dinner. I actually don't remember that part, because as had become my habit, I was sneaking shots of vodka from his alcohol cupboard. Before I knew it, I had drunk the entire bottle. When the bottle was empty, I decided to put it in my overnight bag, and then the next time I came over I would put a new bottle of vodka in the cupboard.

A couple of hours passed, and we decide to go to bed and watch a movie. My boyfriend was looking for the remote and went over to the chair where my bag was sitting. Instead of finding the remote, he found the empty bottle of vodka. The bottle was not inside my bag. In my drunken stupor, I had put it next to my bag, and he found it. He kicked me out and said he was done with me. I drove home, which I really should not have done. My younger sister was living with me at the time, and I went rushing into her bedroom crying, hoping to be comforted. All she said was, "So what are you going to do?"

What am I going to do? I thought I had tried everything,

and there was no hope for me. I was desperate to figure this out. Once again God was telling me to stop. Why would I listen this time? I sat with my tears of desperation asking God to guide me to sobriety. I didn't have any more fight in me. I was in the dark night of my soul. I was lost, tired, and hopeless. I sat for what seemed an eternity. When I woke up the next morning, the sun was coming in the blinds, and I felt comforted and peaceful. God had spoken to me once again, but this time I listened. I knew in my heart and soul that I didn't have any more chances to drink.

I put one foot in front of the other and marched into an AA meeting. I walked in and surrendered. Nothing had changed about AA, but I had changed. I was finally ready to do the work.

I listened and followed what fellow alcoholics had advised me. They suggested I go to a meeting every day for the first ninety days. Get a sponsor to take me through the twelve steps of Alcoholics Anonymous. Work the coffee bar; it is a fantastic way to meet sober people. Get involved in the AA club.

I genuinely believe that God led me into surrendering to the principles of AA. I had to get out of my own way and do the work. Was it easy? No. Was it worth it? Yes.

I now have a relationship with God, which is very new to me. I was raised in a Catholic family, and my relationship with God was always hierarchal. I knew a few prayers and that was good enough. I did not know how to talk to God until someone taught me to "talk to God like you do a friend." That made sense to me. On any given day you can see me talking away with my best friend, God. I know he is there because there are so many wonderful things that have come into my life that I cannot explain, and I do not even try to understand. They just are.

My sobriety date is June 28, 2015. Every day since, I do this thing called life, one day at a time.

Reflection

When you've hit rock bottom, what choices did you make and how did those choices transform your life? Would you make those same choices now? What changed due to your choices?

How are you getting in your own way and what's one thing you could do to make a shift? By when will you make that shift?

Do you celebrate an anniversary of a date you made a significant commitment to yourself? If you were to celebrate, how would you do so? What's stopping you from celebrating?

PART TWO:

Life Purpose

The Urge for Going

CARA HOPE CLARK

I've developed this uncanny ability to know when it is time to move on throughout my adult life. As a result, I have grown accustomed to the all-too-familiar stirring sensation, trusting that my higher wisdom has a course correction in store for me.

My most recent call to action came after seven years of living amongst the stunning mountain scenery in Boulder, Colorado. Its heavenly beauty captivated my heart from the moment I arrived. I remember declaring, "This is it; I'm never moving again!"

However, the Universe had other plans for me.

I stepped out my door each morning with my sweet little eleven-pound sidekick Lyra, a white terrier mix who loved walking and hiking just as much as I did. Boulder Open Space Trails were within a five-minute drive, and just a seven-minute walk brought us to a park with a lake encompassing unparalleled views of the iconic Boulder Flat Irons.

I often thought that the mountain skyline looked more like a paper cutout pressed flat against the vast Colorado sky from this vantage point. With its seasonal grandeur, this backdrop provided me with a limitless supply of essential healing support and joy.

As the external world became engulfed with lockdowns, I valued the gift of this respite beyond measure–my calm in the storm.

One cool sunny day in early 2021, perched on my favorite rock overlooking the lake, I heard the message, *you are no longer in alignment with Boulder; it's time to move!* I thought, what the heck, there's no way! This is crazy on so many levels!

Until that day, I had no clue that living in Boulder had an expiration date.

Much to my dismay, this higher calling would not release me, though I tried repeatedly to ignore it.

Resistant, I questioned, "How would all this seamlessly come together?" I was already at my wit's end with deadlines to publish my book *Widow's Moon*. The enormity of navigating a complex move on the heels of that seemed unimaginable.

Ultimately, I conceded that despite this perspective, and my emotional attachment to my friendships and surroundings, it had become energetically uncomfortable residing in my previously held sanctuary. A mere two weeks after publication, I surrendered to that insistent clarion call. I knew without question that living in a home with acreage, and the solitude it would bring, had become a necessity for my wellbeing.

Craving a softer, lusher feminine landscape, I decided to move to Asheville, NC. In my previous life before Boulder, we had a home there that was used as a vacation rental. I fell in love with Asheville's natural beauty during those six years. Though I didn't live there full-time, I imagined that it would feel like going back home to a place that had brought me peace and contentment.

Finding a new home in another state with a tight housing market was dizzying. Still, I held on as best I could as that roller coaster ride sped into its final destination, with all the puzzle pieces magically falling into place.

From a higher perspective, I can now see that every detail was perfectly orchestrated from start to finish. However, while caught up in that grueling process, it felt immensely challenging to trust that it was all working out for my highest good.

After a mere two and a half months, both exhausted and exhilarated, I landed on my tree-lined perch, nestled on six acres. As if waiting for my arrival that early November afternoon, I touched down in time to catch the last vestiges of the fall colors. With its unique majesty, my mountain top would be my new roost, giving me solace and renewal. I could finally breathe and know with certainty that this was indeed divinely guided. Phew!

Though I was grateful beyond measure, and I loved my new home, clearly, I needed to recalibrate to this present-day reality. Without warning, disorientation, grief, depression, and fatigue became ever-present. Lost in confusion, I wondered what I had just done and why! I was in a holding pattern as if held captive by the "space between." That place where the "old" no longer applied and the "new" has not yet come into form. From this vantage point as an intuitive, it felt unsettling to be staring into the void.

Within four months, as if awakening from a trance, wondrous synchronicities began to unlock, one by one like falling dominos. The dark spell had been broken. I vividly remember seeing illuminations comparable to lightning bugs, each one representing an aspiring future possibility. Reassured, I now knew that an updated version of myself would gradually emerge.

One of those lights revealed a faint message, *Why*

don't you set up an art studio in that extra room down-stairs? Painting again would be a powerful way to express yourself during this life transition. Other than Process Painting that first year after moving to Boulder, my brushes became temporarily obsolete. On my daily walks, photographing the expansive Colorado skies became my obsession.

As fate would have it, one of my new neighbors, Shela, was an artist. Once she found out that I was also a creative, she invited me to several artist studios and galleries in the River Arts District. Weeks later, she confided in me, "Secretly, I'm hoping to inspire you to get back into your painting again."

It worked.

Soon, everything fell into place. The inkling of creating a home studio in Asheville became a reality. Shela suggested that I join her for an Art2Life online course. I initially felt hesitant due to my long hiatus from painting, but the "yes" was so strong I couldn't ignore it. The intense buzzing of excitement was almost too much for my physical body to hold. On a deeper soul level, I sensed that this might be the impetus for many of those future lit possibilities seen months before. My newly resurrected painting journey was officially underway!

Finding myself poised at the threshold of multiple converging events, I understood the multifaceted reasons the Universe delivered me to Asheville. From that level of clarity, I freely welcomed the gifts on behalf of my soul's evolutionary charge.

In addition to passionately re-engaging with my art
and moving back to Asheville, 2022 marked the tenth anniversary of my husband's suicide (as mentioned in my story "Ready or Not" in *Life Reimagined*). Just a month later, I welcomed my sixty-fifth birthday. With age comes wisdom. I sure have earned it!

Though my grief will always inform my path moving forward, I permitted myself to untie the heavy cloak of that intensely transformative decade and the preceding sixty-five years of a life well-lived. Holding a renewed slate, I honored all my past selves and knew that this season was ripe for new beginnings. My golden opportunity came with a unique sense of freedom in letting go, which I must admit felt a bit foreign and at the same time invigorating.

As the vibrant colors of spring emerged, I asked myself, "Do I still miss Boulder? Yup! Do I wish I could go back? Nope." Between the increased wildfires since leaving and my growing curiosity and fulfillment with what was blossoming in my new world, it was clear that I was where I needed to be.

If I had ignored my urge for going, I would have remained frozen in the security of the known. My new future would have simply passed me by. I wouldn't be holding the potential of a life newly infused with emerging opportunities for happiness, creativity, connections, adventure, and maybe even love!

I believe that our seemingly crazy and unexpected impulses to embrace change are the soul's language, guiding us to our greater and fullest expression of who we truly are.

Sometimes the most potent transitions are the ones where we have no idea where we will end up. That's where I do my best to lean into courageous, radical trust. I am grateful that I allowed myself to look beyond my perceived limitations. Stepping onto the path of co-creation and partnership with my higher self, I have learned that facing fear, change, and uncertainty helps us come alive. It is the breath that our soul requires.

49

Reflection

How are your attachments to the safety of known holding you back from creating the life you have dreamed of? If so, what inspired actions can you take to release those perceived limitations?

Our soul asks us to take a leap of faith when we hear the call to embrace change. What changes have you felt inspired to follow?

Trusting your higher wisdom, what steps can you take to move in the direction of your soul's desire?

Awakening
My Soul's Path

AMY KNOX

*I*n March 2022, the virus had shut down the world, but I was beginning my midlife journey. I enrolled for the Southern New Hampshire University online bachelor's program to receive my degree in psychology with a concentration in mental health. I was about to start my life's true path at age forty-seven. Not only was I going back to school, but I was doing it online. How was I going to navigate through this technology? I was educated by attending classes, not by computer. My nerves were on high alert; I was partly excited and partly scared. This was not an easy decision. I didn't just wake up one day in March and decide to go back to school. In fact, my path to returning to college was fraught with many detours.

In high school, I thought I had my life planned out. I wanted to be a successful businesswoman. I was not sure what that meant, but it was a goal. I planned to move away from my small town, live somewhere fabulous, travel the world, and be the best at my career. Well, that did not

51

happen. I went to a community college and worked as a waitress. During that time, I met a man who gave all his attention to me, and I fell hard for him. He had goals for his construction career, and a love for being adventurous, and we shared many laughs, which I had never experienced. One year later, at twenty years old, I was pregnant and getting married. Talk about my life doing a one-eighty.

I didn't finish college (I was one class short of receiving my associate degree), I was living in the same town, I had a family, and I was working full-time for benefits. I had my second child at twenty-three. This was not what I had envisioned at all. I focused on being the best mom and wife I could be, and I put my dreams on hold. My husband and I managed to open a roofing/sheet metal fabrication business that became successful and was beneficial to our family. I was able to be a stay-at-home mom while helping out with our business. It was a wonderful time, but I knew I wanted to do more. I knew I was meant to help others. I felt a constant tug to change direction. I had internal battles daily about leaving my convenient position in the family business and starting all over from scratch. What about the kids? Would my husband understand? So many obstacles were in my way. I kept my thoughts locked up and my emotions under wraps, but each day that I did not act, my true self was dying just a little bit. I would envision different scenarios for my future, always wondering what it would be like to live out my heart's desire.

Whenever I would take one step forward to change my path, I became good at making a thousand excuses as to why I shouldn't. I would listen to the voice that wanted to protect me from failure. That voice would tell me, "*You are not worthy*," or "*Don't make waves in your otherwise still life.*" The self-sabotage of excuses protected my ego, but my soul paid the price. Once again, I was unhappy. Days went on, months turned to years, and my children were growing up. I was not doing myself any service in not acting on my dreams. In fact, I was doing myself a big disservice.

It's funny how one thing can impact your life forever. In 2009, I found out about working with crystals and how you can incorporate them into your everyday life. I thought this would help with how I was feeling, so my best friend and I took a crystal class to broaden our awareness of other holistic modalities. That's when I ended up finding my mentor/teacher, Lisa "Ishwari" Murphy, who helped uncover both my gift and my life's path. Through her energy medicine classes based on natural law, and indigenous practices, my idea of life was blown to bits. She took me from being unconscious to conscious. I had been walking around in a fog when I thought I had complete clarity. I found my voice; I stopped being a people pleaser; I stopped being in roles that others put me in. I created healthy boundaries.

With this work, I also had to explore my shadow side. I had to go through the dark to get to the light. It was an extraordinary process. I learned to feel again instead of being behind a wall. I had no idea that I was disconnected from my body because of traumas that occurred when I was younger.

Through this healing, I unveiled my gift of communicating with the spirit realm, along with discovering a love of sound meditation and a desire to help others to find their true path. I couldn't stop exploring these new avenues of the alternative world. I became a Reiki Master, and I continued on to be certified by the International Institute of Reflexology. I began apprenticing in energy medicine classes. I also found I had a unique skill of helping people transition over, a Death Doula. What an honor to ease a person's soul of fear and let them move on with grace.

53

Awakening My Soul's Path

With this newfound knowledge, I also created a better home life for my husband and children. My children have been on transformational journeys too. Life has moved upward. Once I had started my own holistic part-time business and had clients, I desired to offer more. I wanted to go back to college and finish that degree–but not in business. I wanted to learn more about our spirit, and our brains and behaviors, by majoring in psychology. This was part of my destiny path. I could feel it in every bone in my body. My heart sang at the thought of accomplishing my bachelor's degree. I knew this was the right path.

It was not easy to go back to college. My mother-in-law was diagnosed with Alzheimer's and had to be placed in a memory care facility. I was working full-time at the family business and part-time for myself, along with taking ongoing educational classes with Lisa, and I had a household to run. In a world of chaos, it can be easy to slip into its clutches and spiral out of control. Lisa taught me that by staying in rhythm, flowing with my own energy, and staying connected to the pulse of Mother Earth, I would be able to accomplish it all. It would be a daily practice; a test of my will as to how much I wanted this. I would have to ignore the egoic voice that so wanted me not to continue.

I had complete faith in myself, despite heading into uncharted waters. I enrolled at Southern New Hampshire University, where they accepted my transcripts from 1993, and I started off as a junior. I would achieve my goal in two years! I dedicated myself to studying and didn't give up when times were hectic. My mother-in-law's condition worsened, and she passed during this time, which was difficult. But I stayed in my connected practices, and I actually completed college one semester early. How did I maintain this place? By staying in my own rhythm and not getting caught up in others' advice about how I should do things.

In December 2021, I graduated *summa cum laude* with a bachelor's degree in psychology. What a feeling of accomplishment to know I was on my way to fulfilling my dreams! The voice that tried to protect me could not speak. Instead, I listened to my heart, and I succeeded. Next, I will attend graduate school, where I fully intend to obtain a PhD. During my studies, I will share with others the healing journey that Lisa "Ishwari" Murphy guided me through. I will blaze a path in psychology, while teaching others about how to work with energy, including how sound therapy and other natural healing modalities can transform your life in such a short time. Just like how Lisa saw my spirit and talents, I too want to bring consciousness back to those that have been unconscious. Together, we will let their light shine like a hundred thousand bright suns.

Reflection

In what ways does your shadow side or your childhood traumas keep you locked behind a wall of defensiveness? Where can you allow yourself grace to explore these, and how would doing so change your life?

Have you ever felt disconnected from your body? What did that feel like, and what actions did you take to reconnect to it? Describe the process and experience.

Where in your life can you instill boundaries that support you? What resistance could come up, from you or others? How can you counteract that resistance?

The Journey from Lost to Found

CLAIRE K CROFT

I don't remember where I lost myself, but I do know when I chose to be found.

The day started like the others before, tears replaced by a smile, the mask that hid the truth. I was an actress in life, a chameleon, constantly molding to blend in, be accepted, and be liked. The *yes* girl, when my body screamed, *NO*. From the outside looking in I had it all: a loving husband, three inspirational children, a beautiful home, a thriving business, and yet inside I was lost, alone, and desperately sad. The signs were there, recurrent cold sores, constant headaches, and bone wearing fatigue. All ignored and masked.

I had grown accustomed to living life like a "to-do" list, an efficient functioning robot that was slowly malfunctioning at the smallest of triggers. The trigger on that day was not hearing my son, Sam, say "bye" as he set off for school. I tore down the stairs and ran through the driving rain in a desperate attempt to wish him a lovely day. But he was gone. I prided myself on being a good mother, and I felt like I had failed.

57

The Journey from Lost to Found

Ella said, "He'll be back soon, Mum." Her eyes revealed the truth: she saw through me.

I swallowed my tears long enough to smile as she and Lucie headed off to school. As the door closed, a wave of emotions cascaded over me washing with it the armor I had held onto. I slid onto the cold floor; my knees hugged into my chest like a baby within a womb. Numb, broken, but not alone. Lying alongside me were fragmented pieces of me, the unloved, the unworthy, the suppressed, and the starved. I had run, but I could no longer hide. My light extinguished; in truth, I wanted out. A presence greater than me lifted me that day, along with a clear knowing that things were going to change. *I was going to change.*

The days, weeks, and months that followed were uncomfortable, vulnerable, and raw. The realization that I had been alive, but I had not been living. I got honest, took responsibility, and began asking hard questions. *Who am I? Isn't this the life I wanted?* A beautiful family, a Victorian home with whitewashed wooden floors, high ceilings, and open fireplaces. So *why* did I feel the home that once hugged me, close in around me, why did the pressures of a large mortgage engulf me, and why did my marriage feel like a ball and chain? A wildly disorientating time, and yet, I felt more empowered and alive than ever before. I was no longer the *yes* girl, the doormat, the submissive; I was in the driving seat, with one destination: to feel happy and free.

I needed space, time to heal, and time to rediscover myself. I took mini breaks alone, just me and my unloved parts. If I was to feel whole, I needed to stop hiding from myself. These breaks, which were an unsettling time for my family, were not always supported or understood, but they were accepted. Being a master of the mask meant no one knew how broken I had become. My children called me Mummy Sunshine. They saw the light in me, before I did. I owed it to them to ignite, nourish, and own my light, so they could own theirs. I know my husband, Pete, was hurting. His world had turned upside down, but I didn't have the bandwidth to support him, the words to explain it, or the reassurance that all will be okay. Truth was, I didn't know.

As uncomfortable as it felt, I couldn't go back. I trusted the voice inside and courageously forged a new path. I gave notice on my Pilates studio lease in favor of a small garden studio–a heart-breaking decision to my detriment as I hated letting people down.

I bought a static caravan. An investment that, on paper, made no sense, but for me it was a sanctuary away from the busyness of life. I expect the notion of a midlife crisis was raised, especially on the arrival of a baby blue Vespa with a matching helmet! Giggling at the thought of it, I desired to feel wild and free (spoiler alert–*turns out you don't get that from a bike*). It was a rather messy middle, a period of releasing, experimenting, and replenishing, but a crisis this was not. It was more of an awakening; to live life as me, for me. I became a happiness seeker, a magnet to books, courses, tools, and spirituality.

The more me I became, the more I realized how disconnected I had always been. *As a teen, I had starved myself; as an adult I had starved my life.* If my life was to flourish, I needed to nourish it, love it, and be in the experience of it. The way I lived became my medicine. The more I gave myself, the more I was able to give. The more present I was to life; the more magnificent life became. The more alive I felt in myself, the more alive I was for others. The more connected I was with myself, the deeper my connection to all. The smile that was once a mask was real. People said I looked different. I *was* different, my robotic self was loved back to life.

The ripple effect of my newfound joy for life was

seen, felt, and mirrored. Happiness shone from within. Tears pool as I picture Pete smiling as he looked at me. He had given me space when he wanted to hold on tight. Freedom when he didn't want to let go. His surrendering opened room for his own healing. We were both growing, thankfully together, rather than apart. I healed. He healed. We healed. Our children were spreading their wings afar, armed with life lessons beyond their years. Who knew that being selfish was the most selfless act I could perform?

When I was lost and unhappy, I filled the void with meaningless stuff. Now, I dreamed of a simpler life. Less space, less stuff, less pressure, and more time. Living through the pandemic reinforced that. I held a fantasy of living on a houseboat, at one with nature, with passing ducks as neighbors. Pete and our youngest daughter Lucie were not 'on board' with that reality, but they were open to change. My dreams became our dreams. Dreams became plans, and plans were actioned. With logic in the back seat, our hearts led the way.

We sold our family home for a two-bedroom apartment by the sea. I anticipated some well-meaning opinions on this interesting choice for a family of five and two dogs! But, surprisingly and joyously, we only received love and support. Confirming that love will always be mirrored back, even if not understood. I had shed emotional armor, and then I shed stuff. It was the best detox I have done. Warmed by the joy of giving, I delivered, gifted, and donated a lifetime worth of belongings. Standing in our echoey kitchen on the last day felt strange. Our worldly possessions fit into one van. A pendulum swung between exhaustion, relief, sadness, and excitement. Tears of gratitude fell for those soul-hugging walls and marked the end of a chapter.

I type these final words sitting in our light-filled apartment, the sound of passing seagulls added to the gentle snore of our contented dogs. I feel overwhelmed with love for myself, my family, and our commitment and devotion to life. Not only am I living a life I love (*we* love), but I am empowering you to claim and live yours too.

This story spans over a rollercoasting seven years. Every loop to loop, twist, and turn, all the lows, and highs, were worth it. I am free to be me, wild, untamed, quirky, and FUN me, my armor replaced with wings. How wide they expand or how high they fly is not yet known. Fun and adventure are on the horizon. The only question is, will we hit the open road, or venture out to sea?

This is the *beginning* of a new chapter for me, for you, for *us.*

Reflection

Your body is communicating all the time. What has yours been telling you? Where is your body crying for attention?

Be curious of the masks you are wearing. How are they serving you? What identities are you ready to let go of?

What would living a simpler life look like, *feel* like? What action(s) can you take today to simplify your life?

This is the Lifetime

EMILY MADILL

I sat on my porch, basking in the warmth of a heat dome that hung over the Pacific coast. It was the last day of school for my sons, and I was enjoying the warmth and solitude while taking online classes to renew my coaching credentials. Sea-glass windchimes danced in the balmy breeze, and soothing sounds from my outdoor water fountain matched how I felt inside.

This calm, though, would be short-lived. I didn't realize it then, sitting on my porch, that the next twenty-four hours would be heart-breaking, each hour becoming worse than the one before.

The message from my brother came out of the blue. *Michelle has had a stroke.* The words didn't make sense. My sister-in-law was the youngest adult in our small family. She was healthy and fit—and a good friend, ever since we'd been roommates when I was in teaching school. I'd introduced her to my brother all those years before, and they in turn had made me a very happy sister-in-law and auntie to two beautiful nieces.

I immediately drove to the hospital. Even though I

63

was in a state of confusion, I managed to speed through every green light like my life depended on it. If we hadn't been in the middle of a global pandemic, I would have run through the doors of the ER. Instead, I sat in the parking lot, frantically trying to figure out what was going on. The hissing sound from the air conditioning was more than my nerves could take. Strands of hair blew in my face. No one was answering my calls or texts. Just as I was ready to rip my hair out, my mom answered. Michelle and my brother were getting helicoptered to another hospital. Michelle needed emergency surgery after a blood clot caused a stroke.

At that point, it didn't seem real. My focus was to get to my mom and be there for my nieces when they got out of school. But the moment we reached my house, we received instructions to get in the car and drive to the hospital a couple of hours away. Michelle's surgery wasn't going well.

The hospital made a special allowance for us. My nieces, nine and twelve, were able to see their mom one last time. My heart cracked open when my brother told my nieces their mommy was going to die. It was a devastating and pivotal moment.

The hours, days, and weeks that followed moved in slow motion–except there was so much to do and so much of my energy to give. A massive meteor had landed on my family, causing a crater-like void that needed to be filled. This void, though, was impossible to fill, even for a nurturer like me.

I was so intent on softening everyone else's pain that I often forgot to tend to my own. In the beginning, my only safe haven was the shower. There, I could ugly-cry as the sounds of the water drowned my pain. I was safe to not inconvenience anyone with the sheer agony I was feeling inside.

I kept juggling the different parts of life, never daring to slow down for fear I would fall apart. So many people relied on me to keep myself together. At least, that's what I told myself.

Before Michelle's death, it had been years since I'd felt a pain that brought me to my knees, and a lifetime since I had given myself permission to fall apart. Back then, I'd put myself back together, moving forward with a sense of purpose, and recovering my inner compass and source of calm. *But what if this time was different?*

Michelle entered my life twenty years ago after another shattering loss: the death of my close friend Danielle. She was killed by a drunk driver on the way home from an evening of dancing. Home from college, I had begged Danielle to come out that night. In the weeks and months that followed, I was overcome with waves of shock, rage, and remorse. It took years to forgive myself for not staying in that night with Danielle.

The shock of sudden loss and deep regret I felt shook the inner compass of who I was becoming. At the time, I was in business school with loose plans to go into accounting. After Danielle's death, that no longer felt right. I found a way to transform pain into purpose by changing gears altogether and following the intended path of my beloved Danielle, who had been born to be a teacher.

My teacher training gave me the experience to write children's empowerment books and curriculum, and, later, to build a business I love. Danielle's memory was with me at every step, reminding me to lighten up and follow my dreams in my own unique way. *This is the lifetime!* she used to say. Boy, was she right.

I think I've always understood that life is temporary, a gift we may not receive tomorrow. When I was just six months old, my dad died in an accident, and the heightened emotion surrounding that event instilled in me the belief

65

that life moves forward even after hard things happen. That my mom could endure it with strength and grace has shaped what I believe about the human spirit and our resilience in the face of tragedy.

I've been told that my dad was adventurous and athletic–a tradesman, but also a creative who loved to paint. And I've always sensed my dad with me when I write. Over the years, my relationship with words and my impulse to translate them into something meaningful are other ways I've transformed pain into purpose, even unconsciously.

My history with loss hasn't made grieving Michelle any less painful. I know that the enormity of such a loss has the potential to ruin the lives of those left behind, to rip families apart. Grief is a strange beast. Each milestone in the first year can feel like one step forward, two steps back. But I'm more determined to make every step count. It's okay to fall apart and to rebuild from where I am. I have done this before, and I can do it again. These are the words I tell myself.

It's been an arduous walk for my small family. It's also been a heart-opening and eye-opening one. We weren't ripped apart–we were brought closer together. We all have our moments, but we aren't ruined. We are alive.

This midlife shakedown has become my wake-up call to live each day like *this is the lifetime*. In order to find my way back to my inner source of comfort and calm, I don't give my yeses to anything that feels like a no. I view my time and energy as cherished resources. Family is my priority, and raising my teenage sons, as well as supporting my brother in the raising of his girls, is an honor and gift I don't take lightly. Getting to create and serve through my business fills my heart with purpose. I don't put my energy in anything else that doesn't add to the equation in a positive way.

Six months after Michelle passed, on Christmas day, I recertified my coaching credentials. Christmas was her favorite day. I felt her cheering me on, encouraging me to fully step into my light as a coach. She was always a cheerleader of women stepping into leadership roles. She instilled that leadership potential in her daughters.

Integrating this loss one day at a time has strengthened the inner compass of who I am—who I have always been. I feel Michelle with me when I sit on my porch and listen to the birds sing. I feel her when I'm with her daughters and the wind rustles their long amber hair, when the sun shines on their faces, when they tilt their chins back to let out a hearty laugh. Perhaps it's the memory of her, or a hint there is more to life than meets the eye. Either way, I lean in and allow these special people I've lost, who've touched my heart so deeply, to join me on my journey. Living life to my fullest, one word, step, and exquisite day at a time.

Reflection

How has the loss of a loved one changed your perspective?

In what ways might you be staving off joy because you're afraid of loss? What might change if you allowed yourself to feel joy despite the threat of loss?

Have you ever experienced feeling the spirit of someone who has passed away? How did they show up and what did it feel like for you?

What Are You Waiting For?

SUSAN OPEKA

*J*ournal entry from September 3, 2005: *"Here's a question–how do you know when you feel you're being called to do something - like have your own business - vs. just reacting to a trauma? I'm still searching. And I can honestly say that what I'm doing for _____ isn't what I want to do. It's not about her; it's about me. There's no spark and I can truly say I'm not sure why I'm doing this. I think I yearn to have my own business. Couldn't I have a store that helps women? If I don't do this now, when will I? Why wait? Why force myself to keep doing something I no longer have to do? This has become almost physical for me. I just want to help people feel better."*

When my mother died in August, I had to transition from being her caretaker, to planning her funeral and cleaning out her home to… going back to "living." Only now, I wasn't sure what "living" looked like for me.

Career-wise, I was excellent at what I did for a financial consulting firm, and I made a great deal of money as the major breadwinner in my family. I had steadily advanced in my thirty-year career, and I was proud with the progress

69

I'd made.

But was I happy? Did I love what I was doing?

For years I dreamed of having my own business; of putting away my briefcase and doing something mean- ingful. I had a burning desire to help others. It showed up when I was a corporate leader who sent inspirational quotes and books to my team. And it showed up again when I moved into the consulting world and developed close relationships with my clients. I found myself doing the same for them—sharing quotes and inspirational books. I loved being of service in that way. It lit me up inside.

Yet that was only a small portion of my job. Did I have the guts to walk away from it and pursue something that lit me up all the time? My mindset was one of fear mixed with wondering, and fear continued to win out. I journaled constantly about what I was feeling, looking for insight and answers from Spirit.

Then my mother had a debilitating stroke. It was easy to decide then; I resigned from the consulting firm so I could care for Mom and be her medical advocate. When she passed away three months later, I had a big hole in my life that needed to be filled.

Another consulting firm doggedly pursued me. It was easy to just accept their offer and get back to what was comfortable and familiar. Only I was bored most of the time and had little enthusiasm for the work.

The little voice in my head became relentless. It kept at me, asking me if I was doing what was easy or if what I was doing was right for me. "Shut up!" I'd say. "Just let me be!"

It didn't shut up. In fact, one day, after I'd been with my new firm for three weeks, I was in my car, sitting at a red light when the voice started up again. "I'm ignoring you," I said. *Okay,* it said, *just one last thing.*

If not now, Sue, when? What are you waiting for?

That night I wrote the journal entry at the beginning of this story. It was part catharsis and part plea for help. I knew I was at a breaking point, and I started to melt the ice around my fear. I decided shortly after that entry that I was giving myself permission to stop having a job and to start having a life.

I read somewhere that successful people have several things in common, among them that they trust their intuition, have patience and faith, and take action. So, I started to keep a dream book. I wrote down anything that came to mind that felt good and that I could see myself doing. No surprise, a major theme emerged around my passion for helping others, particularly women, feel better. I kept at it, searching for the idea of what that might look like.

Re-reading that journal entry from September was an a-ha moment for me. Retail had appealed to me my whole life (I used to play store when I was six years old), and it made my heart soar thinking of a place where women could come to be nurtured and uplifted.

What about a store that sold uplifting, meaningful, and inspirational items? And, what if it also had a bookstore with big comfy chairs, hot tea, and lots of inspirational books? And, what if I offered workshops? The ideas were coming rapidly, and my excitement continued to grow.

Another hallmark of successful people is that they can visualize their success and take action. Once I secured in my heart the idea of this store, I could see it in my mind. The Universe helped me by leading me to a space for rent in the exact town I wanted to be located in. I easily found a designer to help create the look and feel I had imagined, and I located a contractor through a friend of a friend.

We opened a few months later and quickly became known not only as a great gift store but also as a place to go to feel safe, listened to, and relaxed. We became a destination for women who needed a great gift or a touch of inspiration. Sometimes a person would stop in, take a deep breath, and say, "Ahhh, I needed that," and then leave! These kinds of comments, plus watching the pleasure on my customers' faces, validated my idea and dream.

Looking back, I know that my mother's passing was the reconnection I needed to reignite me to my purpose. I will be forever grateful for that.

You could say I also proved what we know to be true about the Universe: when you are clear about what you want, the Universe will bring it to you. I used to tell people I could see my store so clearly in my mind when it was just an idea. The Universe helped me to bring that picture into reality.

Journal entry from mid-2006: *"I realized today that I don't ever have to buy another suit if I don't want to and do not have to renew my subscription to CFO magazine. Yeah me!"*

Reflection

What in your life do you've regret not doing, and how has
this regret affected your life? What are you not doing
that you want to?

Have you ever heard that voice inside speak to you?
What did it say, and did you listen?

Describe an a-ha moment you've had.

The Lady of the Lake

LEE MURPHY WOLF

*W*e can put your program on pause...I understand...if you change your mind, I would be happy to work something out with you...."

I hung up and gasped, like I had been punched in the gut. The room began to spin. My limbs felt heavy and numb. The unthinkable had happened. My business had collapsed.

It was March 2020. My husband and I were at our lake house to ride out the pandemic. Just a few days before in a panic, we had packed everything we could fit in the car, leaving our life in New York City behind.

At fifty-three years old and after seven years as an entrepreneur, this was not how I thought my life would be. Suddenly, I was untethered from everything I knew. A wave of grief swept over me. How could this have happened?

Every day was monotonous. I'd wake up, stumble out of bed, and scroll through the news. Then I'd reach out to friends and peers, longing for any semblance of normalcy. We'd listen to each other's stories and cry. Then I'd stare at the lake, check the news again, and play out scenarios about what I could have done differently. I'd go to sleep aching and empty.

One morning while sipping coffee on the deck, I saw a family of ducks, float by. They glided across the water so serenely, not a care in the world. As I watched them, my breath became deeper, and tension melted from my shoulders. I wanted to be like those ducks.

That summer, I started spending more time on the lake. Some days I'd paddle to the lily pond in my fuchsia kayak and drift through the reeds, imagining I was in India. Other times, my husband and I would hop on our boat and "tour" Europe, pretending each cluster of homes was a different country. Then we'd pick a quiet place to drop anchor and take a dip, gently floating on noodles and bobbing with the current. In the evenings, we'd sit on our deck and watch the sun set.

There were no thoughts, no distractions, and there was nowhere to go. Time seemed to stand still.

As I immersed myself in nature, my senses reawakened. I heard the brightness in a robin's song. Knew what time it was by the flow of the current. Felt the clouds billow like freshly spun cotton candy. When the breeze brushed my skin, I crackled with electricity. I felt more alive than I had in years.

That's when she came into my life.

At first, I could not see her, but I could feel her presence. She came one morning when I was having my Akashic Records read. She felt warm, safe, and wise. When she was around me, I didn't feel alone.

The more I opened to her, the more she showed herself, appearing as waves of red light then as swirling green and yellow spheres. Eventually, I could see her full form. She had long, flowing red hair and a mermaid's body.

She called herself The Lady of the Lake. When I asked her if she was my Guide, she said, "Yes."

Intuitively I knew I could trust her. I spoke to her daily after meditating, or when I opened my records myself. She comforted me when I felt overwhelmed. She sat beside me when I felt lonely. She validated my hunches. She even laughed at my jokes. She became my constant companion.

When the summer was over, I felt rejuvenated and hopeful. I mustered the courage to ask her what was next. I itched to be useful and to be of service. I had ideas about a mastermind I wanted to offer and felt good about the direction I was headed.

Her reply caught me off guard. "You are a healer."

Exasperated, I thought to myself, "No way!" I had been split between business and personal development, swinging back and forth like a pendulum for years. I never wanted to be in the healing arts. Nor did I want to go back to school for intense amounts of training.

I had always been drawn to a more creative and soulful life, but never believed I could make a living at it. I built my entire corporate career and my success as a business coach making decisions based on what made strategic sense. I was paid well and was good at what I did. But deep down, I knew there was truth in what she said. I longed to do something different. But healing arts–that was edgy territory. It scared the shit out of me.

My rational mind kicked in to ease the sting. "Maybe this is your chance to start over," the mental part of me said. "It's an opportunity to do something you'd be really passionate about."

My ambivalence shifted moment to moment. Sometimes I'd imagine myself hosting intimate retreats, and it was exhilarating. The next minute, I felt agitated and anxious. I needed clarity. I sensed that the answer was not going to come from my mind. I had to go deeper.

The next time I was in a reading, I decided to go with

77

no expectations and see what happened. I dropped deep into my heart space. I heard the honking of geese as they flew over our house. I remembered the ducks from earlier that summer, picturing them gliding across the water, and took a few deep breaths, slowing myself down to their pace. I asked The Lady of the Lake, "What am I to learn today?" I had never asked her such a simple question. She answered with a richness that took my breath away.

I asked her this same question every time we connected. Each time, she shared small bits of wisdom and gave me a glimpse of what my future could look like. It felt pure and true. I started to relax and believe that something magical was about to unfold, and whatever it was, it was the best next step.

When she felt I was ready, she told me to work with tuning forks.

I was stunned. I never had a tuning fork session, nor did I know anyone who worked with them. I had lots of self-care rituals and received hundreds of other wellness treatments over the years. It was totally bizarre, something right out of left field.

I knew immediately in that moment that I had to try it.

I bought a cheap set of forks on Amazon. I had no idea what I was doing and started experimenting. From the very first strike, I felt a vibration in my hands that moved through my entire body like a warm wave. It was sheer joy!

I practiced daily on myself. For the first three weeks, I was woozy after each session, as if I was drunk from absorbing the frequencies. My dreams became more vivid. I woke up mentally clear every morning. I rediscovered the language of my soul as I healed myself.

I felt ready to look at the bigger questions in my life. Should we sell our apartment? If we did, where should we go? My husband was a dyed-in-the-wool New Yorker. Would he be happy? What would people think if we left?

The Lady of the Lake started showing me visions: me barefoot on my deck, clients coming to see me for sessions by the lake. Snippets of a lush tropical backyard with a pool and small sound studio. Me hosting retreats at the beach. It made no sense but felt right.

We decided to sell our New York apartment and move to St. Petersburg, Florida. I culled through listings and followed my instincts with the Lady's guidance. We bought our townhome online, based on a grainy FaceTime walkthrough.

I kept following my passion. The more I tuned myself, the more inspired I became. I started to study and felt a desire to share my knowledge with others. My first offers took shape. Some worked; others fell flat. My passion became my inner GPS.

The more I trusted my inner wisdom, the less I saw her. By the time we moved to Florida, she stopped visiting me. Being in nature and tuning myself brought me back into harmony. She is with me, always. Even if I can't see her. Because she is a version of myself.

Reflection

How do you connect with nature and in what ways does it rejuvenate you? Do you spend enough time connecting in this way? If not, where can you expand this connection?

When and how have you taken a big risk to change your life? What did you learn about yourself through this process?

In what areas of your life are you like a pendulum, and how has it affected you?

The Journey Toward Wholehearted Alignment

DONNA DUFFY

*T*he next level of growth would take our company to $500,000 in revenue. We had our eyes on the summit and we were steadily climbing with each passing year. August 2016 arrived, my birthday month, brimming with hope and possibility. Yet, by mid-month, we had lost our highest paying client. That pop in our monthly revenue left me at a crossroads. I could hustle to make up the difference or open my hands and let it go.

Soon began a dismantling of all that we had built. At fifty-six, after years of hustle and grind, there seemed to be nowhere to go but up. Yet with the loss of that client, I found myself reeling back from the hit it meant to our bottom line and to going forward. I felt deflated and defeated. We had put too many of our eggs in the same basket and had not build up our pipeline. Where to go from here?

In looking back, I see I'd gotten off track. I'd traded

my passion and purpose for ambition and accolades. The heady ascent was like having a lack of oxygen while scaling a summit. I was not thinking straight. The thrill of the climb and getting there caused me to forget the values I held dear and soon, I was on dangerous slopes, heading straight for a crevasse I didn't see coming. I didn't understand alignment then like I do now and couldn't see that I was being beckoned by the Pied Piper promise of "greatness," which would eventually exact too high of a price from me.

At first, it felt like I was in a free fall, wondering what just happened. One minute I could see the peak, the summit in clear view. Just one step, then the next, and we'd be there. Until we weren't. That misstep was just the tipping point. We had been heading toward this precipice for some time, but I hadn't calculated on factors that would have given us a better understanding of the lay of the land.

The morning after we'd lost our client, I penned a blogpost, a note to myself and a clarion call to other women, "The Power of Resilience is in the Speed of Your Recovery: Get Back Up." This became a mantra to guide me, a talisman to guard me, as I navigated my way forward. It reminded me what mattered most and propelled me forward with greater wisdom and understanding, a quest toward greater congruence in my life and work.

What today looked like a kick in the teeth, would tomorrow be a cherished gift, and I had to be brave enough to push through, to tell myself the truth and get back up. I learned that my resiliency was reliant upon my willingness for recovery, to not just sit in what happened. I was determined to move forward with grace and dignity.

The next few months brought deep soul searching and the decisions that emerged altered the course of my life and business. Some days I spiraled, and it seemed like the bottom was falling out. I found myself dredging up my greatest mistakes and deepest regrets as I raked myself over the coals.

At times, I felt I had reached the end of the road and that I was failure and fraud, asking myself who would want to listen to me anyway. I needed to tell myself the truth: to keep going, one day at a time, one step at a time. With deep trust in God and a renewed sense of calling and purpose, we moved forward.

We held a "Between the Trapezes Party" as a milestone for us and our local business community. It was our way of saying that we were leaving one place and moving to another. We gathered in our spacious office suite as they wrote well-wishes and heartfelt sentiments across our twelve-foot whiteboard wall. And with that came the end of a chapter. We downsized the space, the staff, the events, and my sense of identity as a leader.

We decided to go compact for greater impact and what seemed at the time as a major disruption, loss, and failure, would eventually be seen as a welcomed lesson and gift; a reprieve and an opportunity for reinvention.

That sacred moment called for courage and a will-ingness to be brave enough to open my heart to what was possible. It was time to open my hands and let go, not only of an address, but my idea of how my business journey was supposed to be, so I could receive something even greater and more wholeheartedly aligned for me.

At first, I thought I would be letting everyone down. But to not shift and embrace this new pathway would be letting myself down and that would have been too high a price to pay.

I believed then that success meant scaling up to the bigger office suite and staff, to attaining, achieving, and acquiring what seemed like a rite of passage for the next level of growth in business. Now I see it all very differently.

Loss is a great teacher.

Instead, I decided to do things in favor of myself and the life and business I wanted to create. I decided to niche down to primarily serving midlife women entrepreneurs, to lean into deeper, more focused work and grow the Sage Success Studio business and community.

To step into wholehearted, single-minded alignment, I had to have the courage to choose wisely, again and again, making micro choices that led to mastery. In time, I learned that greatness had nothing to do with fame, fortune, or the number of followers and fans we had. Greatness would be wrought from the unswerving willingness to fully embrace my God-given gifts and do the kind of work that nourished my soul.

As I let that vision take visceral root in my heart and soul, choices became easier because the decision to live and work like this, has already been made.

It's not by default then that we get where we want to go, it's by design. It's not by accident but by intention.

And yet, there were thing that kept nudging me out further to the deepest most aligned parts of myself, beckoning me to take another step.

I'm thrilled that now in my sixties, there is still more to do, be and create. I think of the times that I have barred the door for fear of what's on the other side. But now, I find myself flinging doors open, passageways and corridors of courage and possibility.

The resistance especially at my age is much greater than it has ever been. Long gone is the starry-eyed, twenty-four-year-old, rucksack on her back, holding all she owns, out to change the world as I ventured to Europe and then the Middle East.

Or is she...?

No, she's still here. I'm still here! Maybe with more creature comforts that I could carry, but just as much hope in my heart. And now I have an even better map than I did then, and a compass that points true north.

Now, with the decades behind me, I hold the souvenirs of all that I've accomplished, weathered, and survived. I move forward with less naïveté and more wisdom. In place of quest toward ambition is soulful sojourn toward greater authenticity and congruence.

Now, I go forward with more confidence, not only because I know what I'm capable of, but what God can do in and through me as I stay true to myself and the work I'm called to do in the world.

Marriage of a decade gone. Babies born, grown, and gone. Houses lived in and moved on from now gone. What remains? Everything that matters.

Relationships with grown children deeper and ever-lasting. Living with myself that once seemed impossible now an everyday life that is cherished and deeply appreciated. The letting go of possessions, prestige, position for the sake of being seen which was so much about me, and in its place the welcoming of instead being found.

With a deep sense of coming home to self, I come bearing the gifts I've been blessed to share with a tribe of women I feel honored to serve, not allowing those things in that will bring discord and misalignment. Signature work that lights me up, learning to say, all else is no.

Reflection

Donna found herself on a climb toward her next level goals that seemed to be within her grasp, until it wasn't, and things began to unravel. Can you think of a time when your expectations on what would happen next, and reality collided? How did you recover?

Donna shared her "Between the Trapezes" event to signify the transition of going from one place to another, one chapter to another. Can you name one "Between the Trapezes" moment in your life or work?

How have you seen resilience and tenacity in your own life and work? Name one time when you were at the crossroads and could have given up but decided instead to get back up.

PART THREE:

Relationships

Manifesting the Love of My Life

DEBORAH KEVIN

*M*y high school sweetheart, Rob, began appearing repeatedly in my dreams in the spring of 2021–thirty-one years after we last saw each other. Although I couldn't see him, I knew his energy and that he was desperately trying to tell me something–I just didn't know what. When I mentioned these appearances to my intuition mentor, Nicole, she asked key questions that helped me hone in on what was happening.

Rob and I had a long history, meeting at sixteen then dating for two years in high school and college. He abruptly broke up with me in the fall of 1982, shattering my heart. In 1987, we reconnected, moved in together, and got engaged. By the spring of 1990, I knew the relationship wasn't working and broke off our engagement, shattering his heart. We grew our separate ways until he began appearing in my dreams.

On June 15, 2021, in a guided meditation session with Nicole, Rob appeared again, and handed me a scroll. As we debriefed the meditation, I said, "I think I'm to write him a letter." As weird as it sounded, especially since I

89

had no idea where he was living or where he was on his life's journey, I knew it was what I needed to do. That same night, after researching the Internet for his mailing address, I sat at my keyboard and wrote a four-page letter brimming with gratitude, jumping into the void that lived between us, offering reconnection and friendship. I put the letter into the mailbox immediately, knowing if I waited, I'd never have the nerve to mail it.

My hope was to reconnect in friendship, but not knowing where he was in his life, I let go of any expectation that he'd write back. I released the outcome to the Universe.

One June 25, my mail carrier delivered two cards with a New Jersey postmark: one saying how happy Rob was to hear from me, and that his more-developed responses would be forthcoming, and the other was a card overflowing with happy recollections about my recently departed dad's life.

I shared the second letter with my stepmother, who immediately asked through a veil of joy-filled tears, "Is Rob single?"

"I don't know," I said, wondering myself.

What unfolded was a USPS dream: snail mail letters filling both our mailboxes as we wrote back and forth for six weeks. He had been married for eighteen years to a woman nine years our senior. When she passed away in January 2018, he buried himself in work to manage his grief only to have COVID hit and his job of twenty years evaporate. At a complete life's crossroads, he turned to Louise Hay and meditation for emotional support.

It was during his deep meditations about me and our relationship that I believe he showed up in my dreams. We had repair work to do together, and we decided to dedicate ourselves to doing just that.

In 2015, I had stepped away from an eight-year

marriage to a man who was physically, emotionally, and financially abusive. I then spent the intervening years going into deep emotional work. I meditated and tapped back into my intuitive gifts. Examined my stories, released subconscious beliefs, and held myself accountable for my choices. When friends asked me about dating, my reply was the same, "I feel like the person I'm supposed to be with is already known to me. I just don't know who that is." I also believed that the love of my life happened early for me and that no one could fill Rob's shoes—so I didn't even try to attract that kind of love. All that changed with the investment in myself.

So, the woman Rob was re-introduced to was certainly not the woman he'd known before. I can say the same about him—the big heart and loving care still existed and was beautifully augmented by wisdom, grace, and expanded kindness. In fact, when I revisited my MANifesto, a graphic I created to attract my soulmate, I saw him in every word.

As our letter-writing progressed, my graduate school residency and graduation in Colorado loomed on the horizon. I didn't want Rob to think I'd ghosted him, so I provided my mobile number and email address when letting him know my travel schedule.

I was settled into my Colorado AirBnB after a long day of classes when I received a text from an unfamiliar phone number with a 215-area code.

The text read, "Hi, it's me."

I burst into laughter, knowing exactly who the "me" was even though I didn't have Rob's phone number. Over the course of ten days, we texted back and forth and set up a first phone call upon my return to Baltimore. We texted about meeting and floated all kinds of places and ideas, none of which felt right. Instinctively, we knew we'd need more than a few hours together.

Our first call was scheduled for 7 p.m. on a Monday

night. Promptly at seven, my mobile rang. I answered, "Hello." I mean, what does one say after thirty-one years?

My greeting resulted in both of us erupting into uncontrollable laughter for about twenty minutes! And then we talked until three in the morning. These late-night calls happened every night for the first week, during which time I invited him to come visit me for a weekend.

"I'm here," his Friday afternoon text said.

I smoothed out my dress, checked my hair, and tried to calm the thumpty-thump of my heart. What would he think of the fifty-eight-year-old me? I ran down the stairs of my Co-Op and turned the corner just as he reached the end of his van. A smile split my face, mirroring the smile on his. I would have recognized him anywhere! I ran into his arms, both of us hugging and crying in an embrace that lasted what felt like an eternity. There was no awkwardness, simply ease and joy.

That weekend led to us seeing each other every weekend. We talked about the past, cried over shattering each other's hearts, brushed away the old debris, and reveled in our present selves. Our families greeted the news that we were seeing each other again with joy and acceptance–which we didn't need but certainly were happy to receive. My sons said they'd never seen me so happy or heard me laughing so much–and they both wanted that for me.

As Rob and I rededicated ourselves fully to each other, we were handed shocking news. On October 5, 2021, I learned I had breast cancer, which required several surgeries, chemotherapy, and radiation.

Immediately, Rob cleared his schedule to attend every doctor's appointment. He turned his life upside down to be my caretaker post-surgery. I never once worried about his reaction to my scars or drains–his loving care and energy set the tone for my recovery. When it came time to shave my head, he took the clippers from Michael, the hairdresser, and made the first cut up the back of my head.

"I can tell this guy's a tender and loving person. Most men would have shaved from the front. Rob chose to start at the back," said Michael, taking the clippers and finishing the job.

Eight months into the cancer journey and Rob is still my biggest advocate and encourager. For Christmas, instead of material gifts, he offered me monthly getaways, so I had something fun to look forward to. We've been to art showings at the Brandywine River Museum as well as Harry Potter and Van Gogh exhibits in Philadelphia, we've hiked in Shenandoah National Park, and have Paul McCartney and Barenaked Ladies concerts to look forward to.

We also made the decision that Rob would sell his house and move to Baltimore. We used our intuitive skills to manifest a perfect buyer and, as I write this, that process is fully underway.

There isn't a day that goes by that Rob and I don't express our deep gratitude for each other, for having the courage to write and respond, and invite back into our lives the deep, lasting love we have for each other. We laugh easily, trust completely, and know that this gift we've given each other will last every day for the rest of our lives.

And so it is.

Reflection

Describe a time in your life when you had a deep knowing about something. Did you act on it? If so, what transpired?

How have previous relationships informed your other relationship choices?

Where can you lean more deeply into your intuition and how might doing so serve you?

A Widow's Journey from Darkness to Light

CAROL BILODEAU

You will be alone.

As I walked down my stairs, this premonition flooded me. It weighed so heavily on my soul, I couldn't begin to imagine what it meant. I immediately put it out of my mind, until several weeks later, I learned what this premonition signified when I received a call from my husband's boss, telling me that my husband had collapsed at work and was being transported to the hospital. That day changed my life. The premonition had come true: I was alone.

Our life together was one that you'd see in commercials—always together, supporting each other, holding hands, and in love. After searching for over thirty-three years, I had found my soul mate.

We met at the office. I first thought he was a stuffed shirt in his three-piece pin-striped suit! It wasn't until we worked together that I realized he was much more than that. We spent time talking about family as he was about to become a part-time dad. I realized he was a kind and gentle soul. At year-end, we worked closely together to ensure our employer's products were shipped. Later that evening, as snow gently fell and glistened in the lamplight, he walked me to my car and kissed me. It was the type of kiss that curled your toes. It was at that moment, that we knew we had a connection. Less than a month after that moment, he asked me to marry him, and we married one and a half years later.

In 2004, we relocated to Nevada. We made the decision during a snowstorm. We both had grown up in New England and it was time for a change. We packed up our home and went on our great adventure with nothing but the proceeds from our home sale and our dreams.

We made our new home in Henderson and found jobs a year later. In October 2006, for our twentieth anniversary, we renewed our wedding vows with our daughter and son-in-law standing up for us. Again, I had a premonition that we shouldn't wait for our twenty-fifth anniversary. At that time, I didn't understand why my soul was pushing me to renew our vows.

In February 2007, we received a call from a dear friend who had been diagnosed with cirrhosis of the liver. Jimmy was like a big brother to my husband, and we felt this was his good-bye call. Little did we both know that four days later, my husband would be the one making the transition.

My husband transitioned on March 1, 2007. An aneurysm stole the love of my life, and I was left numb and alone. The days that followed were a blur of making arrangements, calling family, and having friends fly in from the East Coast for support.

One afternoon, my daughter told me that her dog Dutchess, who never barked or whimpered, was sitting in front of her, whimpering to get her attention. My daughter asked the dog if it was Dad, and Dutchess licked her face. No matter when Dutchess saw me, she was always excited, but not that day. She quietly laid at the bottom of the stairs and I laid down in front of her, looked her straight in her eyes, and asked if it was my husband. Dutchess took her paw, laid it on my forearm, and licked my face. I knew that my husband was still there, and he wanted to make sure we knew he was okay. Since then, I knew that he could reach out from the other side to help and guide me.

In the fifteen years since my husband passed, I would sob myself sick and then he would send a sign that he was still with me. Losing my soul mate, best friend, lover, and confidante was the absolute worst moment in my life. I had lost both my parents, my only sibling, and some friends, but nothing prepared me for losing the one person who made life worth living.

It has been a struggle to reinvent myself over the past fifteen years, I was in my mid-fifties, trying to figure out who I am and what I want to do with my life as a widow. I was no longer the other half of a couple, but alone again. Working helped, but the deep dark hours of the night alone in our bed was another matter. Some nights, I cried myself to sleep.

This year, on the fifteenth anniversary of my husband's transition, and my seventieth birthday, it became clear to me that it was time to start living again. It was time to stop lamenting and wishing to go home.

My meditation room had become a mausoleum, covered with pictures of family and friends who had passed away.

One Friday morning, I decided to release this weight. I slowly took each picture off the bookcase and held it in my hands. I remembered all the times with this person, thanked them for all their wisdom and love, and wrapped their picture in tissue paper and placed it in a special box. This process took me all day. Saying goodbye again evoked joyful and sad moments, but I had to clear this energy. I did keep one special picture of each person and set up an altar on the top shelf. Now when I meditate, I'm not lamenting all my losses but reveling in the beauty of my space. This was a big moment for me. I've been living in the past so much.

I also decided to release all the medical records of my husband's transition. It tore me apart to read how hard his medical team worked to keep my husband alive.

It is through this process that I've been reborn. I don't mean to sound trite, but the weight was lifted off my soul so I could move forward in my life.

I've learned so much in the past fifteen years, such as embracing the experience and releasing it to the Universe. I also learned that it's fine to cry and lament over a loss, but it's not fine to hold on for years or decades. We all need to cry to release the angst and sadness that embraces our soul; don't feel sorry for doing this. It's part of the process. To get better, you must go through the grief to see the beauty of the other side.

It's the other side that brings you joy and happiness. It's the other side that forms the new you! If someone tells you differently, ask them if they've gone through it. If they have, then ask for their input; if they haven't, then dismiss what they've said. Only those of us who have gone through the trials of widowhood know what it's truly like.

If you're a widow, this is not a club you entered willingly, but the Universe deemed that it's where you belong. Don't beat yourself up. Treat yourself lovingly. It's okay to be sad, and it's okay to cry. Let it go, pound the pillow and ask why. Sometimes, the Universe will give you an answer, and sometimes it won't. Just go with it until you see the dawn of the new day. Trust me, you will see it! Whether it be in two years or fifteen years, it will come. It is there, and it will be where you are born again.

Namaste.

Reflection

How has holding onto memories stopped you from moving forward in your life? What actions did you take to bless and release those that no longer served you?

Have you ever had a spiritual connection with a deceased loved one? How has it manifested itself in your life?

Describe your grieving process. How has Carol's story impacted you in terms of understanding your grief, expressed or unexpressed?

Unraveled

CHRISTINA WAGGONER

Shaking as I gasped for air between the inconsolable sobbing, I threw myself onto our bed and pulled my knees into my chest, making myself small. The inner turmoil felt like a gripping in my gut, and I was terrified that I might fall to pieces right at that very moment! I pulled even harder on my legs, desperate to shrink into the tiniest possible version of myself. Our twenty-fourth wedding anniversary was only a week away, and I felt desperate! We had built what started as a beautiful life together on a foundation of friendship and love. So much had transpired in those twenty-four years together.

But the memories of that strong connection faded fast as the marriage rapidly unraveled. Our connection had diminished to sleeping separately and barely acknowledging one another. All the playful, fun times were a distant memory. I tried so hard to hold it all together. The nights were the most challenging time, and I barely got by, especially after the kids went to bed and things got quiet. Sleep escaped me as my mind raced. I hated myself for letting things get so miserable. I spent most nights

figuring out how to fix things between us. My thoughts often led me back to our early days together. I yearned for the way he used to look at me. But this night was different, due to the all-consuming terror I felt because I knew that I had to fully come to terms with what had happened and make the toughest decision of my life.

I will never forget the first day we met via a mutual friend. My friend and I sat on the couch chatting, and I leaned over to tighten the laces on my boots. A moment later, I felt a presence above me. The energy of this presence was strong. Something shifted within me. It was as though time slowed to a crawl. My eyes first caught sight of his brown alligator skin cowboy boots. I swallowed hard, and my gaze slowly traveled up to the tattered hem of his well-worn button-fly Levi's and white Ralph Lauren knit sweater. Then, my eyes continued their upward path to his prominent Adam's apple and chiseled jawline. I noticed every detail of him, including his tanned nose and cheeks. I was totally absorbed in the exploration, and it continued until our eyes locked and it seemed as though time stood still. His eyes were the most beautiful ocean blue I had ever seen.

He uttered one word in the most charming, masculine, southern dialect. "Howdy."

My heart leaped into my throat, and my cheeks flushed and burned. "Hi," I said. It was love at first sight, and I was hooked. At that moment I decided that he was the man I would spend the rest of my life with. The twenty-plus years that followed had many highs and lows that we helped each other through. However, toward the latter part of those years, a looming concern about the true strength of our marriage had developed.

We all have our inner struggles from time to time. He often called his inner struggle his demons, a somewhat common term that some people use to describe the constant nasty chatter of the mind. I never wanted to call it that, as it felt too scary to think of demons being in my mind! He never liked to talk about what his demons were. The perpetual fixer in me wanted to know and desired to help and repair whatever was causing upset or inner turmoil for him.

I had inner struggles too. It was excruciatingly painful facing my inner struggles, most of which came from self-doubt and insecurity. I didn't feel good enough, smart enough, or worthy of life's best. I sometimes used alcohol as a soother of the inner chatter. He was also my best friend and had become my soother. He knew everything about my family and me. He knew and understood what I feared, and he seemed to know just how to help me, a skill I was incredibly grateful for! I loved him, and so did my family. I wanted to be his soother, too, but he preferred alcohol and cigarettes.

As I hit my forties, I decided that feeling good about my health and well-being would take precedence over the chemical soothers. I decided that for myself, and I decided that for him. I now recognize that was part of the unraveling of our commitment to one another. At the time, I didn't realize that it might not be my place to try and solve things for him. It was not my place to fix him. It was his decision and his job to make his own choices, fulfilling his own journey.

Over time, I feared that his demons and soothers were gaining control over my life. I feared the effect that the soothers could have on our children. This led us to an ongoing battle. I always thought it was me battling him, and, in a big way, I was. Our arguments could be vicious at times. In truth, I really was battling his soothers. I worried about him. I worried about what our future would be like if he could not soothe his demons. I worried about what life would be like for our children and us. He didn't want

me worrying about him. In fact, he just wanted to be left alone to do what he wanted to do. The man who I trusted as my husband and best friend began to distance himself from me.

Things had come to a head between us on that heavy, moonless night, and I was gripped by a fierce intensity of emotions–fear, self-doubt, and uncertainty. I now realize that I had lost my own inner light that night. I didn't think I had the courage and strength to walk away from everything we had built together. But I also knew that I was rapidly shrinking, which felt as though my soul was slowly being crushed.

I called out for help, but no one answered. The bedroom door was closed; I was alone, my voice weak. I thought that no one had heard me. But, as it turned out, God was listening. Something shifted in the depths of my despair, and I felt a glimmer of hope, or what I would now call my true self. I felt a sense of peace wash over me. The crying and shaking stopped as my muscles relaxed, and I rolled over, clutched my pillow, and drifted off into a deep, sound sleep.

When I awoke, I knew I had to leave my marriage. I still had a long journey ahead of me, but I knew that I could do it. I would make the break and move forward alone. And I promised myself that I would hold my head high and become a better version of myself.

Coming to terms with what I thought to be my biggest failure was the most significant challenge that I had ever faced. However, the decision to end our marriage was also the foundational step that gave birth to my transformational growth, physically, spiritually, and psychologically, which has led me onto a beautiful, rewarding trajectory to find, and be, my best self.

Reflection

Have you ever experienced "love at first sight?" Describe what happened.

Describe a time when your inner light felt extinguished and what you did to relight the wick.

Share what you consider to be your biggest failure. How can you reframe the experience to see the gifts brought as a result?

Holy Moments

ELAINE BLAIS

The giant door closed behind me as I stepped into the sunlit Barnes & Noble store. Scanning the shelves, I spotted the book I was looking for–a recommendation from a friend. But something else caught my eye. Tentatively, I slid *Spiritual Divorce* by Debbie Ford off the shelf. I'd never thought of divorce as spiritual. It had been eighteen months since my divorce; I should have been over it. I bought the book and headed home.

On the drive, I replayed that painful last goodbye. Standing in the shadows, arms around each other, the familiar warmth of our bodies pressed against one other. I had been relieved to call it quits. Nevertheless, as we parted, I had felt my life rip into before and after. I had held myself together, not wanting to let go, but knowing I must. I had fought back the tears, with finality pressing against my chest as the door closed on thirty-five years of life together.

I had also closed the door on all those years of putting everyone else first and setting my dreams aside, thinking I was selfish. I believed I was wrong to want them. I had everything: good husband, beautiful children, house, career. The dream. *I should have been happy. What was wrong with me?*

When my children left home, I'd begun dusting off those dreams. At fifty-two, I'd returned to college to complete my degree. I'd started volunteering and I created a community of friends who were open and curious. The more expansive I'd felt, the more I did things I longed for, the further apart my husband and I had drifted.

At home now, I made tea and curled up on the couch with my new book. I wanted more than anything to feel whole again. As I read the introduction, I sobbed. "Divorce is a holy moment." I'm challenged to see the gift.

My daughter is angry with me that I left her dad. My family seems indifferent to what I'm feeling. They invite my ex to family gatherings, but no one asks how I feel about it. *How is this holy?* Feeling lost and alone, I pretend to be okay.

Pretending is what I'm good at. I was a little girl with big emotions–smart, curious, and logical. I grew up with violence, lots of anger, and a mandate to be nice. I'd always felt different, beyond my parents' ability to manage or understand. "Because I said so," and "stop crying or I'll give you something to cry about," silenced my questions and feelings.

Wrong and shut down, I learned to pretend. I focused on pleasing others to avoid blame, shame, and punishment. If I could just be what they wanted, then they'll love me. Stuffing my anger deep inside, I believed I didn't matter. The oldest of five children, I was often left to watch my siblings while mom ran errands. When things went wrong, and they did, I was blamed. "You should know better." It seemed my family only loved me when I was good, nice, and compliant.

As I continued reading my new book, I journaled

feverishly, coming face to face with this part of me: The pretender. Pleasing. Nice. Perfect. Trying so hard never to disappoint anyone–all to avoid the pain of rejection. I began to see the pattern. Divorce is bad. I am bad. I failed to be perfect and get it right. My deepest fear is that no one will love me. *This is a holy moment. I am blessed by this divorce.* I keep repeating these words again and again through the tears.

I realized I am just beginning to grieve this divorce. No more pretending. Now the observer of my life, I see how each step on my life's path has led me here, to this moment of self-insight and understanding I had no idea was available to me until now.

I journaled my life backwards. If not for divorce, I would not know these pieces of myself that have longed to be loved and accepted. I would not be reframing divorce or my life, questioning everything I've believed about myself until this moment. I read the chapter on forgiveness. It felt so hard letting go of blame and forgiving myself for wanting more than I believed I was worthy of.

Slowly, I touched the anger buried deep in my bones. I allowed myself to scream and punch pillows. I wrote angry letters, then forgiveness letters. I burned them all in the fire of freedom and self-worth. I surrendered to the moment and invited curiosity back into my life. Peace took the place of anger as I found myself in between who I was and who I am becoming. Becoming seems possible now as I allow compassion for the one person, I have neglected most in my life: Me.

Over the next couple of months, I ride the waves of grief and possibility. I grieved the woman I was and celebrated her strength and beauty. I mustered the courage to find my way back to me. I embraced that curious, sensitive little girl and honored the strength it took to navigate her life situation. She brought me to this moment of self-acceptance.

I've come to see all of my life as a gift. Every moment, a holy moment. Now, instead of asking, "Why me?" I ask more empowered questions of myself. "Does this choice or action support the life I want to live?" or, "Who do I want to be, and is this in integrity with that version of myself?"

I trust my intuition, and my choices. No matter the outcome, I know I have my own back. I no longer shame or blame myself for anything. When those feelings come up, I slow down and feel. I curiously seek the wisdom of my body to guide me, knowing I am safe to meet my needs. It is safe to be me.

I give myself permission to be the "me" I so deeply craved as a girl. I am more compassionate with myself and have greater compassion for others, including my parents. I know they did their best to love me through their own unresolved pain.

Life gives me exactly what I need to live into the fullness of who I am here to be. Sometimes it's an unpleasant kick in the pants. It took me a while to accept the gift of divorce. Nevertheless, it has been one of the greatest gifts of my life, guiding me home to myself and the courage to make myself and my dreams my priority.

Listening to that inner voice and picking up that book changed my life. It was the beginning of transformation and adventure in my life that seemed unimaginable at the time. I continue to use curiosity to guide my life and stoke the fire of self-worth. I am committed to exploring the inner reaches of what is possible and following what feels like joy.

I never imagined this would be my life today: a midlife troublemaker, a disruptor of my status quo, breaking cycles of shame and self-abandonment in midlife. I completed my studies, claiming a bachelor's degree at age fifty-six. In celebration, I went on a solo trip to Italy. Six months later, I exited a long corporate career intent on creating this next chapter of my life on my own terms. I took a chance on me once more, certifying as a life coach and creating my own private practice.

Stepping into more of who you are meant to be, doesn't come without fear or apprehension. I've found the best way to move through fear is to get curious about it, thank it for wanting to protect me, and then to trust myself to know what to do with confidence and grace. That includes trusting myself to love again, and I've met an amazing man and together we rise in love. I'm also planning my next adventure with a mobile lifestyle.

My purpose now is to empower other women to give themselves permission to dust off their dreams and step out of the shadows of shame and self-abandonment, make themselves the priority in their life, and stand tall in the glorious nature of who they are here to be. It is a joy and blessing, and a dream awakened.

This is what that curious, sensitive little girl came here to do. This is why I am here. It is never too late to be who you truly are.

Reflection

In what ways are you pretending to be who you think you should be?

What patterns can you see that keep you from expressing your true nature?

Where could you invite more curiosity and compassion into your life? What shift could result for doing so?

Taking Care of Home Plate

KATHY SUE LEWIS

I had my children at a young age, which meant, for me, that I should set aside any ambitions and goals of my own. You see, I thought that being a mother was always about putting my children first and making sure that everyone had what they wanted and needed. I honestly thought that was what motherhood was about, not worrying about your own self. This self-sacrifice seemed rewarding at first, but as my children grew older and became self-sufficient, I began to wonder what my real purpose was.

One evening, I was watching a cool TV show about the strange and unusual, featuring a group of white witches. They had a sense of camaraderie, and a connection with the Earth and with each other. They were loving themselves and manifesting and honoring from the powers of nature.

Wow, if this could just be for me, I thought. *I would love to make a connection with others who see the magic and potential in the world that I had missed out on–a sense of purpose.*

That night, while I laid in bed, I prayed I would find

a community of people who practiced magic in their everyday lives... It would be just perfect.

Soon thereafter, my daughter came home from school and was excited about a store she saw on the bus ride home. It had crystals, incense, and all kinds of cool stuff. My daughter wanted to check it out, and my interest was piqued, so when the weekend came, we visited the little place. It was cute and quaint, with crystals and incense. It even had a separate room with Native American items too. Wow, I found my place!

The ladies seemed friendly and were happy to show us around. While we were there, the UPS man delivered a package but needed "cash only" for the shipper. Sally, the owner, opened the register and was short by forty dollars to pay for the delivery. I thought, *well, I came here to spend money,* so I handed her forty dollars without batting an eyelash. Sally was at first hesitant but took the money.

The two of us quickly became friends, and I became an often present, often cash-supplying customer. I loved my friend, Sally, and never wanted her to suffer or do without. I had found my magical friend! I felt needed again as I helped my friend with her many emergencies.

Meanwhile, my spouse's drinking had become a real issue. Although I too liked to imbibe myself, a bottle of vodka a day was a red flag. I learned later he was also philandering with our friend's girlfriend. This marriage had run its course, and it was time for me to get out. He certainly wasn't letting me go without a fight though.

After years of putting myself last in my marriage, I now had the confidence to get my ex out of my life. This was in part because of my friendship with Sally. It was also due to my son, who I knew was brought here to help me. My son was a wise old soul who always had my back. Between my son and my new lady friends, I had the spiritual and physical protection I needed to make this big life change.

As the years progressed, spiritual readings revealed to Sally and me an amazing spiritual place we would co-own. I had stepped into my healing, creative, and magical self. I learned how to make dream catchers and how to heal people by laying hands on them. I had to stay in the background despite my wish for acceptance from others. I let Sally have the limelight because this was so important to her. We were still using her store as our spiritual base, and she liked to remind me that it was "her place." Being in the shadow made me feel important to her, but I also felt like my contributions weren't helping me grow. We made plans to have a new place with healing and retreats, so I tolerated her aggressive behavior because I thought it would get better in our new place.

I learned, though, that my spiritual friend was not there for me. When my mother passed away, Sally was nowhere to be seen, claiming she was too sick to attend the funeral.

As I took care of my aging father, I thought I could count on Sally to help me. However, her emergencies grew and grew, and with every text message, there was another financial fire to put out. I was exhausted, but I kept my eye on the prize: our amazing healing place.

Finally, Sally decided I wasn't replying fast enough and helping her quickly enough, so she ghosted me for six weeks. I became worried about her and tried to reach her, but she did not respond. Finally, Sally called me, reprimanding me for not acting as per her expectations. She had another crisis, and I didn't rescue her quickly enough. For that "misstep," she wasn't going to talk to me until it had been resolved.

I realized I needed to set healthy boundaries and not always allow others' needs to come before mine. I had betrayed myself.

That was our last conversation. Although I felt lonely at times, I realized I was much happier. I also saw that she only contacted me when she wanted something. I wasn't invited for meals or gatherings with her other friends. She also made it clear that her place was hers, and I was no longer part of it. I felt that what I had sacrificed for and worked toward was no longer possible. Sadly, I had to let it go.

With all the financial support I gave Sally, I had dug myself into a complete financial hole. To help alleviate the financial stress, I moved in with my father, who had gotten to the point where he couldn't live alone anymore.

At first, this made me feel like a failure. I dwelled on all the spiritual advice I thought I was receiving from Sally, but I realized she had her own agenda. I had reached a breaking point; it was time to take responsibility and accountability for all of my actions. No one had been forcing me to be so gullible and naive, believing every sob story that came along. My fear of being alone was so compelling, that I didn't think that staying at all costs was the wrong thing to do.

Thankfully, I met a wonderful man, who was understanding of my living situation and always helpful and caring. I had to learn to be open to this type of love and acceptance, and we started to grow together on a spiritual level. The Universe made it clear to me that I was still going to have my haven of healing, and that everything I had built and sacrificed for was about me too.

With his support, I became more and more active in the online spiritual community. I began to make connections with other spiritual people and found outlets for my products and healings. I began to take classes in Reiki, chakra energy, and Akashic records, and even started a spiritual baking company.

I realized that my own gifts and my own self were what

mattered. I also found my purpose: I was here to help others—but on my terms.

What? Something was truly about me, and my hopes and dreams? Yes! I learned it was time to wake up and put myself first. It was time to step into my power and help others to answer their dreams.

My dad had an expression he loved to use. "Make sure you are taking care of home plate." And that's what I am doing. I am using and creating my spiritual gifts and blessings to raise the vibration and frequency of everyone I meet. My lessons continue, and I will grow and learn something new each day—and do so by taking care of myself, first and foremost.

Reflection

In what ways have you placed your needs last?

Describe a friendship you ended, and how it felt to decide to walk away and then close that chapter.

What "alternative" modalities have you used and why did you choose them? How did they support you?

PART FOUR:

Self-Worth

Midlife Flight

CARRIE WOODEN

*T*his is the captain speaking. Due to some minor issues, there will be a thirty-minute delay before we take off. Thank you for your patience."

Well, I thought to myself, *that's not too bad; it gives me time to stretch my legs.* I was grateful for the extra legroom in my aisle seat. I began to settle in when the flight attendant approached me.

"Ma'am, I was wondering if you wouldn't mind changing seats. We have a family with young children, and they would like to sit together," she asked.

I agreed without even thinking about it and walked to my new seat. I was relieved to discover it was another aisle seat, even though it wasn't near the front of the plane. As I settled in next to two young men, I introduced myself and asked their names. Adam was twenty-eight years old, and Troy was sixteen. Adam had just purchased a luxury vehicle and was showing Troy a photo of it on his phone.

I listened in as they continued to talk about golf tournaments and country club memberships. Troy's parents were considering a few different country clubs, and the one Troy liked was $25,000 a year. I smiled and thought to myself, *I didn't even make that much money in the last two years!* I never imagined spending that kind of money on something I needed, let alone something for pleasure.

Once their conversation ended, I asked Adam where he was flying from. He talked about the medical mission trip he had just participated in in Peru. At the end of the journey, the group hiked up to Machu Picchu. Admittedly, I grew a little jealous of his adventures, never considering it in my realm of possibilities. His eyes lit up as he talked about proposing to his girlfriend in that magical place. Adam had lots of pictures to show us.

As we looked through his photos, I felt a longing to experience trips like that but quickly pushed those feelings aside. *I am a single mom with four young children to take care of, and they come first,* I thought.

As Adam explained where the photos were taken and where their next trip would be, I asked where his fiancé was. He explained that they were on standby and couldn't be seated together. Adam pointed her out. She was about seven rows back. She was a beautiful young woman.

Without even thinking about it, I offered to switch seats with her so they could sit together. He was appreciative. As I walked further back on the plane to exchange seats (again), my excitement in scoring an aisle seat toward the front of the plane vanished. In fact, I started feeling quite deflated, though I tried to focus on how I had made other people happy. The young lady, however, was ecstatic that I would be kind enough to trade seats with her and gave me a hug.

Before I could sit down in my new, even-further-from-the-front aisle seat, my new seatmates asked if the husband could move to the aisle seat because his legs were cramping up. His wife moved to the center and left me with the window seat, my least favorite spot on a plane. "Of course," I smiled, feeling a bit defeated. We shuffled around each other, and I shimmied into the cramped window seat. I wondered why they asked *me* to switch seats but had not asked Adam's fiancé.

I sat there feeling sorry for myself while listening to the couple discuss their new business. They also talked about a girls' trip to Hawaii that the wife was taking the next month and a dinner party they were attending the next evening. It seemed that money was of no concern for them. I thought to myself, *I wonder what that would be like.*

I sighed quietly to myself, trying to get comfortable in a window seat with little legroom. I couldn't even recline my seat.

"This is your captain. Please fasten your seatbelts. We are ready to taxi onto the runway and will momentarily be on our way."

The flight attendants began their safety protocols. I watched as one demonstrated how we should always put air masks on ourselves *first* before anyone else. Sadness swept over me.

Why was I sad? Because I realized that for years, I had spent all my energy trying to make everybody else happy. In fact, on this very airplane, I put others' needs ahead of my own, willingly giving up my seat three times and sacrificing my comfort in the process.

My parents taught me to be selfless, serve others, and stop daydreaming, because that was the only way I could make it to heaven. I believed my entire self-worth was wrapped up in doing for others, and I made it my life's purpose. I wanted to make sure I made it to heaven.

With this realization, I thought back over my life and realized I had stopped dreaming for myself years ago. I had spent so much energy each day attempting to make my husband, children, colleagues, and friends happy that I neglected my physical, mental, and emotional health. I

123

was surviving, not living. My proverbial cup was empty. Actually, my cup was broken.

As the plane took off and the cabin light dimmed, I took a deep breath and settled in for the eight-hour flight from Alaska to Arizona. I was grateful no one could see the tears escaping from my eyes. I felt a sense of emptiness I hadn't allowed myself to notice before. I gave myself permission to feel every emotion. I promised myself in that moment, that things would be different. They had to be different! I couldn't keep living life feeling broken and unworthy of happiness.

When I arrived home, I had a full day before my ex-husband would bring our kids back. With this alone time, I began to make a list of what I wanted to change and how I wanted to show up in the world. I didn't want my children to believe that just surviving life was normal. There was more to life than just getting by. I was going to show them that!

The list showed me that I had forgotten how to dream for myself. I knew I had to face my buried emotions. Guilt, unworthiness, shame, frustration, and sadness bubbled up to the surface. I was angry, knowing I had spent half of my life not living in a way that would have been more fulfilling and purposeful. I allowed the tears to flow for hours. I needed that release, both mentally and emotionally. The longer I sat with my feelings, the lighter I started to feel. By the end of the day, I felt a sense of hope and calm, and a willingness to take at least one step each day toward loving myself; to refilling my cup.

I placed my tear-stained list next to my bed so I could easily see the commitments every day. I decided I was just as important as everyone else. Each day for months, I would do just one thing from it. Sometimes that one thing was to allow myself to feel self-compassion. Somedays it was facing my limiting beliefs on money, time, and self-worth, and choosing to believe something different. I added these new beliefs to my list.

Then the day came when I took my tear-stained list off the nightstand. I started a new list. This one flowed with an ease I had never felt. As I wrote down new goals, hopes, and dreams, tears again escaped my eyes, but this time, they were tears of joy, excitement, and gratitude. I looked back over the months with gratitude. I had come so far because I chose to take one small step each day. I thought deeply about how these steps brought me to a place of balance in my life, and peace within myself. I now show up more fully and live with more purpose.

Reflection

Carrie describes her process of listing everything in her life she wanted to change. If you were to write a list, what would be on it? What change would you prioritize?

In what ways have your parents' beliefs impacted your beliefs about what is possible or responsible? Do these beliefs serve you? If not, what can you do to alter them?

In what ways can you invite into your life more self-compassion?

Learning Unconditional Love

KIM TURCOTTE

*I*t was a warm October day, and we were standing in the kitchen when he told me. He needed some space and would stay with his parents for a while. He loved me, but he wasn't sure he was in love with me anymore, and in the final blow, he thought he might be in love with someone else.

If I am honest, we hadn't been happy or healthy for a long time. We were ridiculously co-dependent, but I couldn't fathom a life without him; though we hadn't been great together for years, I had absolutely no clue how the hell to exist on my own, and my entire life felt completely shattered.

I needed support if I was ever going to be able to make it through. Unfortunately, the first therapist I found was less than stellar, and after only three sessions, she told me how great I was doing and that she didn't think we'd need to meet much longer. I remember driving home completely disillusioned and distraught. I knew I hadn't even scratched the surface; I felt lost at sea, and yet it was clear that this woman was not equipped to help me.

Scared and overwhelmed, I had no clue how I was going to navigate it all.

I believe everything happens for a reason, and that day fate stepped into my life in the most fantastic way. About an hour after that session, my phone rang, and it was a therapist I had left a message for when I was initially searching. He apologized for not getting back to me sooner and asked me if I was still looking for a therapist. I told him his timing was impeccable, described my session from earlier that day, and said yes, I was still looking for a therapist.

Over the years, the therapists I had worked with had all been women; I never even considered a man, and seeing a male therapist was scary as hell to me. But after my initial session, my fears were alleviated. Not only did Dr. A feel safe, he felt right, and little did I know in that first session the important role he would play in my journey to self-love and self-sovereignty.

I can't really explain the energy in our relationship, except to say that from the very beginning, there was always a deep respect and knowing between us. He was one of the few people to get me, and this has allowed me to genuinely trust him and to open up to him in the ways that are necessary when doing deep and profound healing work in therapy.

Dr. A was amazing at holding the sacred space for me to feel whatever I felt. He encouraged me to be with the emotions I felt at the surface and, more importantly, to be curious about the emotions I might be holding back. This curiosity and the feelings I uncovered as a result, helped me to recognize all the beliefs that I held around what was okay to feel and what wasn't. It also called attention to who I believed it was safe for me to be and who it wasn't.

All my life, I had always been told to tamp it down, to sit still, to be quiet. I had always been made to feel like I was too much–too loud, too big, too needy, too selfish, too MUCH. But with Dr. A, I felt safe, and we started to explore what it meant to be me. We looked at the me I had kept hidden most of my life–the me I had always concealed out of fear of abandonment, punishment, or rejection. He encouraged me to be everything I was and then some. As a result, I started to trust my feelings, and I was more confident in stepping into who I wanted to be, not who I thought I should be. It felt empowering that I could do this without guilt or shame.

As our work developed, so did my feelings for Dr. A. I remember writing in my journal one day, "I think I am falling in love with Dr. A." I felt so much guilt for having these feelings because, after all, what could be more shameful or forbidden than falling in love with your therapist?

Even though we had explored all kinds of feelings in our work together, I held back sharing my feelings for him. Then at the end of a session one day, I unabashedly flirted with him and immediately apologized.

He looked at me and said, "Don't apologize; this is a safe space, and anything is sayable."

I laughed nervously and said, "Anything is sayable; I like that."

Over the next few months, 'anything is sayable' became our motto, but I still struggled to fully express the deep feelings I felt for him. At some point, I realized that I needed to be completely honest. I needed to meet my fears head-on and speak my truth. I needed to allow myself to be completely vulnerable. I realized I needed to do this for myself, regardless of what his reaction was, so I set out to do just that.

129

Telling him in person seemed overwhelming, so I decided I'd write him a letter. The letter proclaimed my deep love and longing for him. I shared all the things I was feeling and everything I dreamed of experiencing with him. Yes, ALL the things. It was the single most courageous and vulnerable thing I have ever done in my life. It scared the shit out of me, but also felt completely exhilarating at the same time. It was the first time I allowed myself to feel my feelings and the overwhelming fear that came with them, then step through that fear and tell the truth about how I felt. It was unbelievably empowering!

Dr. A handled that letter so graciously. He told me that he had immense respect for me and for the courage it took to share those deep and intimate feelings with him. He assured me, "Your thoughts and feelings are safe with me," and I knew they were.

He also assured me that he cared deeply for me, but that a romantic relationship was not in the cards for us, that it would be an absolute betrayal of everything he stood for as a healer. He told me that he honored and respected me too much to be vague about this, and that he imagined it might be painful to hear. Then he let me know that he was there to support me when I was ready to work through it.

The work we did together after that letter was the deepest work I have ever done in my life. Never once did he ever make me feel anything but safe, supported, and loved. He celebrated the vulnerability and the bravery it took for me to write that letter. And most importantly, he made space for my deep feelings for him to exist, holding the bond we had forged with deep and unconditional love.

That love created a space for me to be able to become whole, to feel safe enough to not only feel all my feelings, but to trust myself enough to express them. I found my voice and I found my power and I felt sovereign within my own self for the first time in my life. It was the single greatest gift that anyone has ever given me, and it completely changed the way I relate to and love everyone in my life, including myself.

My connection to Dr. A, and the work we did together taught me what it meant to be courageous, what it felt like to speak my truth, what it looked like when I broke old patterns and trusted myself and another human being at the deepest level possible. It taught me what complete and utter acceptance and unconditional love truly looks and feels like and it has changed my life forever. It's one of those things that you can never unknow once you know it and it is beautiful. I will forever be grateful for that fated phone call, it changed my life in a way I never would have imagined possible at the time, but that I know was all part of the Divine plan.

Reflection

Describe a time where you experienced unrequited love and how the experience impacted your self-view.

What patterns keep repeating themselves in your life? How would altering these patterns impact you?

How have you experienced unconditional love? How have you expressed unconditional love?

The Journey to Unbecoming

CATHY CASTEEL

I grew up with society telling me who and what I should be, while being raised by a mother who had a tendency to break barriers and labels. Despite my mom's influence, I still had to prove myself to the sports teams that only allowed two girls per team. I hung out with mostly boys to prove I was just as good. I was called a tomboy, and I think deep down inside I liked that label because I wanted to be associated with the strength that society tells us boys have versus society's perception of girls as weak and helpless princesses. These emotions grew into an unhealthy obsession with being competitive.

When I joined the military, less than one percent were female. Being the only female in my unit, and later in my officer basic course, I continued to try to prove myself, ensuring I was not the type of girl that society portrayed. This meant I worked extra hard to be as good, strong, and capable as my male counterparts.

This pattern continued in my civilian career where I once again worked in a male-dominated field, constantly proving my worth and showing how I was not weak and helpless. My desire to be perceived as strong and capable even showed up in my relationships. I did not realize all the masks I had been accumulating in my life just to prove society wrong. I also did not see how I was always proving my worth *to myself*. It didn't help that I received accolades for my accomplishments, which only perpetuated the cycle for more than thirty years.

I left the corporate world in 2013 due to the toll it was taking on my health, going from rarely seeing the doctor to having visits multiple times per week. As I began to shed some of the masks I had worn for so long, it created an unexpected chaos in my life with more health issues bubbling to the surface.

I was left with more questions than answers. What will be the next chapter of my life? Will any of my military reserves experience translate into another civilian skill? If so, what?

I had been working since I was thirteen years old, and now, for the first time in my life, I was leaving a job without having another one already lined up. I sobbed, not knowing what to do. The job paid well, but it was costing my health. Yet leaving with so much uncertainty was not a plan I was sure I was ready to embrace.

For the first time in our marriage, my husband was the only one bringing income into our household. The next two months were a fog, until one day, I started thinking about what I had wanted to do in my life and never did: to become a police officer. How nice it would be to do something for the love of it and not for the money!

Not realizing, I again entered a world where women are the minority and have to prove their worth and value. After having done this for so many years already, I was exhausted and frustrated. One day after my shift, I sat in my car crushed, crying so hard that I had trouble catching my breath. I felt like such a failure. After six months with the police department, I left.

Without the tools I have now, the judgement monster came back to beat me up, "See, you are not as good at you think you are." I am grateful for my husband, who listened to me sob and ramble. He never judged me.

About a year later, I was called to be a servant leader in a different capacity. I had started my journey of self-development. As I dove in, it was like giving water to a person who had been deprived for weeks. I found a fire in me that I had never felt before, and I actually looked forward to each new day and the gifts and learnings it brought me.

On March 5, 2021, I retired from the military reserves with over thirty-one years of service. I didn't realize leading up to and after my retirement, that it would be like slowly peeling off a Band-Aid. While I had changed my civilian life, I still had my military persona–and now, my life as a soldier was over. As I write this, I still feel the emotions I felt the day of my retirement. When I introduced myself to others, I was a mom, wife, and soldier. Now, the soldier part was going away, and it felt like I lost an identity I had built over the last thirty-one years.

When I retired, the desk clerk slid my certificate of retirement and U.S. flag to me from across the desk. That is what my military career amounted to: Documents slid across a desk. To play off the disappointment, I told myself it was no big deal. However, I was sad that this was how my final good-bye would go after thirty-one years of service.

To make matters worse, I was put in for a retirement award, but someone determined that my contribution did not deserve this higher award. I received a lesser award instead. I was devastated because I felt this downgrade reflected a lackluster military career–and others would know it too.

The Journey to Unbecoming

I called my brother, who retired from the military as well, to vent all my frustrations. I am so glad I called him because by the end of the call, I was able to embrace this truth: I know my contribution, and I did not need a stranger to approve an award to validate my worth. *I know my worth,* and it is not tied to a piece of paper.

Over the next year of releasing those identities and stepping into my gift I was put on this earth to do, I realized I was starting the process of *unbecoming.* It's a journey I'm still on today.

I am still working on unbecoming and releasing all those unhealthy beliefs I had about who I was and how my worth was determined. I've entered a chapter in my life where I am showing up how *I* want to show up and not how society dictates.

I am unbecoming all those masks I put on to survive those early chapters of my life, and, instead, loving myself at a deeper level. I am showing up the way I want to and in ways that feel true and authentic to me while also being competitive in a healthy way. Sure, I have cried for what appeared to be no reason, and I have been short or frustrated with my husband and daughter. Unbecoming takes time!

Now I am able to choose, with full awareness, which things no longer serve me, further unbecoming those masks that I no longer want to wear. I learned to give myself grace when those old feelings creep in and embrace the process of living my authentic joy-filled life.

Reflection

What is one way you can implement giving yourself grace each day on your journey?

Write down three ways you show your worth/value.

What is one step you can apply each day to step into your authentic joy-filled life?

Steppingstones

KIM DECLAIR

*W*ho am I? I am a woman, a daughter, a sister, a mother, a wife, a grandmother, and a friend. I am a seeker and an explorer. I have a deep love and appreciation for life. I love nature and this beautiful planet we live on. I believe dogs are earth angels. I believe that the most important thing we can do is to spend our time enjoying life with family, friends, and those around us; sharing experiences and adventures with love, happiness, and compassion. I believe all of life is sacred and an opportunity to grow and expand. I am a Law of Attraction and Life Force Mastery Coach, a Hypnotherapist, and a Qigong instructor. I have a passion for the healing and energy arts, and I feel called to raise consciousness on this planet.

But my story does not start there. I grew up in a wonderful family. Like many families in that era, my father worked, and my mother took care of the kids and the household. I have been told I grew up in a picture-perfect life, and I know that's true. My parents loved and cared for us, enveloping us in happiness, fun, and adventure.

I married young, had a child, divorced a few years later,

and then went to work in the corporate field to support myself and my daughter. I am in a long-standing relationship with the love of my life. I have love, family, friends, adventure, and travel. Life is good.

Somewhere along the way though, I began to wonder: What else? I began to listen to an inner calling that opened up whole new realms, and areas of thought and experiences. For years I followed that calling and encountered what I call my sacred steppingstones–opportunities, directions, and teachings that I believe have been divinely placed before me for my personal expansion and growth.

These steppingstones have been responsible for a lot of personal discovery and introspection. They have also led me to the healing and energy arts, and the desire to teach and share them with others. My father was an educator, and I always believed I too was meant to teach. Teaching and sharing what I have learned became more of those divine steppingstones.

However, I soon discovered that my desire to teach required me to be visible–and in a big way. One problem: I have always been shy, one might say painfully shy, especially as a child. I never felt comfortable putting myself out there. In fact, I have taken steps in the past to stay hidden in the shadows.

So, there I was–a shy little girl who once hid behind her mother, who now desires to move out of the corporate world and share my passion by teaching and coaching. I had a lot of personal growth to embrace!

One of my big a-ha moments was discovering that being shy was not the only problem. I also feared being ridiculed and rejected. After all, the healing and energy arts are not exactly mainstream. Sometimes when I speak of it, people look at me like I am a whackadoodle (especially my husband, who has made no secret that he disapproves of my way of thinking).

To remedy the uncomfortable situation, I started to keep this part of myself separate from my husband and others who *I assumed* may judge me. It was much easier to just keep certain aspects and thoughts to myself. Little did I know that I was creating a big divide and disruption within my being. And I now realize I was not being fair to my husband either. By not sharing my aspirations, hopes and dreams with him, I was not giving him the chance to really see who I am.

At the same time, I started to put myself out there in the teaching and coaching arenas. I stretched, I expanded, I experimented, but I still hesitated to fully step into visibility. That old fear of ridicule and rejection (especially by those closest to me) created a barrier that prevented me from moving forward. I was looping in a pattern of attempting to move forward while trying to keep the peace within my relationship. At times, I even shut myself down and put it all away in an effort to keep the peace.

I gave up my power and created the role of victim rather than stand up for what was important to me. It became a way of life. Keep quiet, yet still do the work and follow my heart. I created a self-imposed prison where I could not be fully me with the one person with whom I should be able to bare my soul. I suppose some part of me thought if I showed my true self, I would be ostracized, abandoned, un-loved and alone. My husband never told me this, by the way, but the fear felt real, nonetheless.

Negative fear hormones coursed through my body whenever I thought my husband might confront me. On a regular basis I lived in fear, which was so contrary to my belief system of health and well-being. I had established this pattern of fight or flight, and I chose flight! I was living separate lives and experiencing split energy. All of this was taking a toll on my physical and emotional well-being.

I had given up my power. No one had taken it from me

because no one has the power to take it from me! I had taken on the role of victim. I allowed what I believed others might think of me to dim my light.

Fast track to when I met Linda Joy and encountered her Sacred Visibility work. I deeply resonated with her, and I remember thinking, "Wow, this is just what I need!" Through Linda I received another big a-ha moment: I am worthy of speaking my truth and openly sharing my thoughts, ideas, and beliefs! I am meant to do this work that I am so strongly drawn to. It is who I am, and if I don't step out, I will be shutting down and losing a part of myself. How liberating that felt!

This new awareness was such a gift because I knew it was time to reach in deep for inner strength and courage, and finally release the fear. By doing the inner work and reclaiming my power, I now allow those closest to me to see and know the full me. I have faith that my relationships will become stronger as a result. And I now honor that inner relationship with myself in mind, body, and spirit.

Today, I choose to follow my heart and do the work I came here to do. I choose love over fear. I stand in my power and speak with the voice of my heart and soul. I put aside my fears and shine my light. I relinquish my self-imposed role of victim. I choose to be me! That is where I find my true joy and fulfillment, and that is how I help others to find theirs. That is how we raise consciousness on this planet.

This experience called life is full of expansion and growth. There are always new lessons to learn, new a-ha moments to experience, and new versions of ourselves to birth. I am grateful for all of the steppingstones along the way, and I look forward to the lessons ahead as I continue that upward spiral of ever-evolving transformation.

Reflection

Where in your life are you allowing people, situations, or life experiences to keep you from standing in your power and shining your light?

What is your current relationship with your whole being—mind, body, and spirit? What steps can you take to integrate and love, honor, and respect those aspects of self?

Are you regularly tuning in to connect with your inner being for guidance? If not, what are some steps you can take to do so?

I Am Sovereign

CRYSTAL COCKERHAM

I found myself in a dark night of the soul as I recovered from knee surgery. I had had surgeries before, but this felt different. Previously, I had found ways to take care of myself, my family, the house, etc., even learning how to be left-handed for a few months.

While this was my knee and I had perfect use of the rest of me, I felt downright useless. I had no choice but to ask for help doing the simplest tasks. I couldn't carry a drink while using crutches, cooking had to be minimal and strategic, bathing and everything else took eons.

Freedom? I felt trapped.

Power? I felt lost, out of reach.

Motivation and energy levels? Zero.

Independent? Ha!

Needless to say, I definitely experienced a spiritual depression. I didn't feel anything like myself.

One of the books I purchased for my recovery was *Dancing the Dream: The Seven Sacred Paths of Human Transformation* by Jamie Sams. It was exactly what my soul needed, and it felt like it was written just for me at

145

that moment of my life. This struggle showed me what I needed to work through, clear, and transform so I could receive, deeply integrate, and embody the matriarch teachings I was about to begin with my mentor, helping me to fully be the woman I am today so that I could help other women through their own spiritual crises.

What I needed to work through may sound simple, however it was anything but. And for those of you reading this who have similar defaults to reset, you know the difficulty I am referring to. I had to dig deep and retrieve those parts of me that had gone unheard for so long: the silent one, the doer, the people pleaser, the perfectionist, and the one whose needs and wants didn't matter. I was and am so grateful for the wisdom and tools I had gained through previous teachings. Without them, and the support of my mentor and community, who knows how much longer, more difficult, and painful this process would have been.

What did these roles have to do with my current predicament? So much! Even though I had done a good deal of personal work already, the doer, the people pleaser, and the perfectionist parts of me were at odds with the silent one and the one whose needs and wants didn't matter.

I couldn't be silent and not communicate my needs any longer. I needed help with daily tasks like housework and making dinner. And I also needed to be okay with things being done differently. I needed to communicate with myself and reconcile the fact that I needed help and then actually ask for it. I reminded myself that nothing and no one is perfect, that perfection is found in the imperfections and in the ability to be fully present. And there were so many old stories that required my attention so that I could finally release them and heal every part of my mind, body, spirit, and soul that called for it.

My spiritual support team was busy! I had nowhere to

go and what I could do was limited, so of course, everything showed up for me at once. There was no more putting myself last, I had to be first. WOW, that was a biggie!

So how did I do it? How did I finally shed the martyr archetype, own my truth, and claim my sovereignty?

I journaled–a lot! I took my time moving through the book I mentioned above, receiving amazing support from my community; more processing, more journaling, lots of tears, and I communicated with myself. This communication then helped me to voice my needs. I no longer remained the silent one. My feelings mattered and I accepted that I was worthy.

This was merely the beginning of my healing journey. The matriarch teachings, that phase of a woman's life when her moon time wanes between motherhood and grandmother hood began, and I was called to also do a piece of work called a vision quest. I look back now at this time that completely rocked my world and laugh in awe of my determination, desire and perseverance to show up for myself, and do my work. Well, when you do that, the work shows up!

I remained motivated, but my energy levels ebbed and flowed. I still didn't feel totally independent, but I was finding my way. Freedom? Power? I still grappled with those, and they just so happened to have been the first part of my journey to claiming my sovereignty and initiating my queendom.

I found myself wanting to be free, free to be me–except the me I thought I was no longer existed. How had or hadn't freedom shown up in my life? Truth be told, I never felt free to be myself. I hadn't had the chance to discover who I was or who I wanted to be in the world. As the oldest of three children and from a young age, I was responsible for my siblings, household chores, their homework, and, on most nights, preparing dinner. Then I had my children young and, while I loved being a mother, I knew I was much more.

Just a few years earlier, I experienced an awakening and a coming home to myself. I also became an energy healer and coach. Yet still, I knew there was more to me than those titles too. I knew I needed to further connect and develop a relationship with myself.

The time had come for the silent one to speak. Time for the doer to find stillness and BE. The people pleaser and perfectionist were relieved of their duties. No longer did they need to stand guard and protect me from anything and everything they considered to be a danger. My needs and wants mattered and, at that moment, it was time to birth myself anew. It helped me to heal, connect, and be with my inner child who had been forced to abandon the freedom of her childhood to accept responsibility. I gave myself permission to stop conceding my freedom and happiness to others, and to reclaim my power.

The silent one found her voice. The doer found solace, clarity, and insight in the stillness. The child was freed. The more I showed up for myself, the more of me I discovered! These discoveries motivated me immensely. My energy levels still ebbed and flowed but were charged with an invigorating energy. I had fun playing with freedom and taking hold of my power.

I spent a lot of time in sacred reflection, forging a relationship with power, trying it on, and sitting with how it showed up in every aspect of my life. Where had I unknowingly and knowingly given my power away? Where did I overuse my power with others? How had I ignored my power in detriment to myself? What boundaries did I need to set with myself and others to not lose, give away, or overuse my power again? What was the most aligned way to use my personal power to stand in my truth and claim my sovereignty at the matriarchal gateway I was bringing myself to?

What I discovered was I didn't have a healthy relationship with power. Meaning, my entire life had been experienced through an incredibly distorted and incomplete lens. This pearl of wisdom became the crowning jewel that brought me fully out of my dark night of the soul and lit the rest of the initiatory path to my queendom.

The preceding nine months resulted in a complete rebirth. The strength in my knee returned in the final stages of healing that took place. To say that I was myself again would be a lie; however, I was no longer the victim, the helpless, the depressed, the silent one, the people pleaser, the doer, the perfectionist, or the one who didn't matter. In all the deep, personal and spiritual work I had gone through, I healed these aspects of myself.

I created a strong foundation to build the rest of my life upon. I knew myself, who I was, and my soul's purpose. Standing at the matriarchal gateway, tears of joy, beauty, and absolute elation joined me as I stepped purposefully and intentionally into my queendom. I am sovereign, guided by the wisdom of my inner light.

Reflection

What books have you read that helped you on your journey? In what ways did they support you?

How has your body reminded you that you had unprocessed emotions or grief?

What does freedom mean to you?

Editor's Note

DEBORAH KEVIN

As I write this note, *Midlife Mojo* is being laid out for publication. Queen Elizabeth II just passed away at ninety-six years old, having served her country for more than seventy years. She did so imperfectly with grace, dignity, and impact–a powerful woman leader in a largely male realm.

Reflecting on the queen's place in history, I'm reminded of the women who authentically shared their stories in this anthology. They've done so to light the way for other women, knowing their challenges can bring hope, believing their *ahas* can spark growth, and hoping that their examples will encourage a new generation of women in midlife to step forward. Because we want–no, we *need*–more women to step fully into their power, to light the dark path of uncertainty, and bravely lead where men fear to tread.

For too long, we've stayed in the shadows, cowed by the patriarchy. Now is the Age of Aquarius, an age of enlightenment. A time for women, all women but in particular those who have reached midlife, to stake their claims, to claim their seats at the table, and to speak their truths. To share their enlightenment with a troubled world. To spread their love and joy and freedom. To be queens of their realms.

The women authors in *Midlife Mojo* share stories of heartbreak, loss, grief, and illness, each trial offering an opportunity for them to transform their experiences, learn from their pain, and grow themselves along the way. May you be drawn to the stories meant to serve you, inspire you, and uplift you. Use the journal prompts to contemplate, excavate, and remediate that in your life which you feel called to.

May these stories bring you to a place of quiet contemplation and then to a place of divine action. The world is waiting for you. Show it what you've got!

About Our Authors

Artist and award-winning photographer **Carol Bilodeau** is passionate about capturing the beauty of nature with her camera. She has earned multiple awards for her photos at the City Lights Art Gallery and various competitions. As an artist, Carol's alcohol ink abstracts, including art prints, coasters, and her popular repurposed bottles, are featured and sold through the Boulder City Art Guild Gallery and other venues. You can learn more at www.CarolBilodeau.com.

Elaine Blais is a personal life coach, midlife troublemaker, author, and spiritual practitioner with a passion for helping midlife women live into their dreams. Using her life experience as the catalyst, she uses a powerful combination of spiritual principles and practical tools to create a way paved with self-acceptance and love for women ready to step into true authenticity and express themselves as boldly as they choose. She offers private coaching, group programs, and workshops. Learn more at www.ElaineBlais.com.

153

As a Neuro-Transformational Coach™, **Cathy Casteel** is passionate about supporting and empowering highly sensitive empathic women to release the layers of false beliefs so they can find their voice, reclaim their self-worth, and begin living the authentic joy-filled life they desire. Cathy intuitively incorporates numerous methodologies to dive deep into a client's beliefs, values, emotions, drivers, and embodied traumas, allowing them to make long-lasting breakthrough shifts in their lives, instead of constantly repeating the same self-sabotaging patterns. Learn more at www.Cathy-Casteel.com.

Cara Hope Clark came into this world during a full lunar eclipse. From a young age, she knew she was more intuitive and sensitive than most. These gifts informed her abilities as a creative and intuitive energy healer. She continues to be a guiding light as the author of multiple award-winning and bestselling *Widow's Moon: A Memoir of Healing, Hope, and Self-Discovery Through Grief and Loss*. From a path well-worn, she shares inspirational wisdom assisting others along their own journey through grief. Learn more at: www.CaraHopeClark.com.

Crystal Cockerham, spiritual mentor, retreat leader and author, works with empathic women to deepen their relationships with the Divine, learn their souls' language, and hone their empathic gifts so they can create the divinely inspired life they envision, desire, and deserve. Through her offerings and community, Crystal empowers and supports women in awakening their inner wisdom. Learn more at www.CrystalCockerham.com.

Lost your way? Aching for direction, passion, purpose, happiness, and fun? **Claire K Croft** illuminates the path of rediscovery, freeing you to see your worth, own your gifts, and manifest a life you love. Claire is a spiritual coach, light leader, energy healer, yogi, writer, mum of three, and ray of sunshine. Her motto is "live life *as* you, *for* you, in service of *all*." You only have one life; make sure it's yours. Live inspired ClaireKCroft.com.

Felicia Messina-D'Haiti is a Master Teacher of Interior Alignment Feng Shui and Space Clearing, Soul Coaching® Master Practitioner/Trainer, speaker, award-winning educator, and contributing author of several best-selling books. Felicia offers personalized coaching, consultation services, and workshops that empower her clients to co-create and experience their own transformation in all aspects of their lives, including mental, emotional, spiritual, and physical. She also offers life-changing professional certification courses in Feng Shui, Space Clearing, Soul Coaching®, and Usui Reiki. Learn more at www.FeliciadHaiti.com.

Applying her in-depth energy and healing arts training, **Kim DeClair** helps women discover the "what's more" to life. Through her coaching and collection of modalities, she guides women to awaken to their authentic selves, embrace their soul's truth so they can honor who they are, and create the life of their dreams. Kim's mission is to raise consciousness on this planet and her work empowering women to live their highest and best fulfills that mission. Learn more at www.Kim-Declair.com.

155

Donna Duffy is a TEDx speaker, bestselling author, and award-winning marketing strategist, offering visibility and marketing solutions to small business owners and entrepreneurs. She is the creator of Sage Success Studio, an online community helping midlife women difference makers showcase their expertise and create their signature body of work for greater visibility, influence, and income. Donna is the CEO/Founder of 3E Marketing Solutions and Global Business Connector for Delaware for the Women Speakers Association. Learn more at www.SageSuccessStudio.com.

With more than twenty years of expertise helping people to transform their lives and careers, **Dr. Colleen Georges** is a life and career coach, TEDx speaker, founder of RESCRIPT Your Story LLC, and author of the eight-time award-winning book, *RESCRIPT the Story You're Telling Yourself*. She is also a Rutgers University lecturer in women's leadership. Dr. Colleen's expertise has been featured in various media including News12, Huffington Post, and Forbes. Learn more at www.ColleenGeorges.com.

Lisa Hromada, Empowered Life*view*™ Guide and Life Transformation Mentor, empowers women to transform their limiting thoughts, emotions, and beliefs into a soul-aligned life of greater joy, self-confidence, and inner peace. Her timeless spiritual teachings and practical Empowered Lifeview™ methods guides women to embrace a spiritual solutions-centered lifestyle, so they can gain the clarity, control, and confidence they need to be happier and more at peace in their lives. Learn more at www.LoveIsTheSeed.com.

As the founder and chief inspiration officer of Highlander Press, **Deborah Kevin** (pronounced "KEY-vin") loves helping changemakers tap into and share their stories of healing and truth with impactful books. She's trekked over 350 miles of the Camino de Santiago and her passions include travel, cooking, hiking, and kayaking. She lives in Maryland with the love of her life, Rob, her sons, and their puppy Fergus–that is when they're not off discovering the world. Learn more about Deborah at www.DeborahKevin.com.

Amy Knox is the founder of Messenger of Your Soul's Blueprint, a healing modality to find your optimal self. With knowledge of energy medicine, natural law, indigenous practices, energy for life coaching and a degree in psychology, she combines them all to find your path. Amy is currently in graduate school, pursuing her advanced degree in psychology, to bring both forms of healing modalities together. To learn more, visit www.AmyKnoxSoulsBlueprint.com.

Since childhood, **Kathy Sue Lewis** has been aware of power energies and entities surrounding us. She has worked for over twenty years honing and developing her natural intuitive gifts and healing abilities. She is a certified Akashic records consultant, energetic acupuncturist, Reiki Master, a teacher of the ways of the runes, a leader of sacred celebrations, and a blessing granter. She enjoys sharing her gifts with others to travel their path on their own soul's journey. You can learn more at www.BlessedBiscuits.co.

Emily Madill is an author and certified professional coach, ACC with a B.A. in business and psychology. Emily is one of Thrive Global's editors-at-large. She has published eleven titles in the area of self-development and empowerment, both for children and adults. You can find her writing in *Chicken Soup for the Soul: Think Positive for Kids*; *Thrive Global*; *The Huffington Post*; *Aspire Magazine*, and others. Emily has a coaching practice specializing in creativity. She supports women creatives and entrepreneurs to sustain their momentum with their project and feel empowered through the process. She lives on Vancouver Island, Canada, with her husband, two sons, and their sweet rescue dog, Annie. Learn more at: www.EmilyMadill.com.

Susan Opeka has taken her passion for helping others feel good and created The Present Moment, a resource center for inspiring people, products, and inspiration. Whether someone is looking for a good book, a motivating podcast, or an inspirational website, The Present Moment has it all. Susan is also passionate about helping fellow entrepreneurs grow their businesses and is a much sought-after business coach and fractional CFO. Contact Susan via The Present Moment at www.ThePresentMomentInc.com.

Karen Shier is a Midlife Transformation Guide, Desire Factor & Law of Attraction Life Coach, energy master, and author who guides women in releasing what no longer lights them up, so they can joyfully thrive in their second half of life. She is passionate about supporting women in moving from feeling stuck, stressed, and unhappy to feeling free, empowered, and ready to co-create a marvelous life. Learn more at www.KarenShierCoaching.com.

Kim Turcotte, ritual priestess, loves sharing her more than twenty years of experience connecting and working with the rhythms of the Earth, the cycles of the moon, and the magic of nature. Through sacred ritual, Kim creates a safe space for her clients to step through fears, trust their inner knowing, and let go of things that no longer fit, helping them forge a deeper connection with themselves and reclaim the sovereignty and self-love that is their birthright. Learn more at www.KimTurcotte.com.

Vera Ventura, a stage IV metastasized breast cancer survivor, is a graduate of Skidmore College and Harvard University. She specializes in mindset coaching, non-toxic living, chemotherapy detox, nutritional healing, and bridging the gap between western medicine and natural/plant healing. Vera is an avid meditator and yoga practitioner, teaching numerous yoga classes and healing workshops. Since 2004, she's been in a 12-step program that addressed all her addictions, whereby she is sober from all mood-altering substances which lead the way for a deep spiritual connection with the divine. In her spare time, she loves watching documentaries about history, traveling, and spending time with her husband Joe, a filmmaker and her two children Alma Vida and Asher. She can be reached at www.BreastCancerGoddess.com.

Christina Waggoner, empowerment coach, coaches individuals ready to deepen their mind/body/spirit connection and desiring to create a fulfilling, joyful life. As a Master Law of Attraction coach, hypnotist and Reiki Master, she combines powerful techniques and processes to support her clients as they release stress and overwhelm and shed self-sabotaging beliefs, patterns, and habits. Her clients experience transformative results feeling calm, optimistic and confident as they step forward into living the lives they truly desire! For more information or to schedule a consultation, please visit www.ChristinaWaggoner.com.

Cindy Winsel, a Certified Creative Depth coach, supports women with depth work, expressive arts, and transformational learning. She uses powerful tools, like Zentangle, JourneyCircles, MoonCircles, and SoulCollages, to allow her clients to experience the many ways they can engage in their own journey. You can learn more about her work at www.CindyWinsel.com.

Lee Murphy Wolf is the creator of The Calibrate Method™ which teaches soul-led, high-achieving entrepreneurs to turn their intuition into clear insights, so they can evolve their businesses. She is on a mission to help them unlock the power of human tuning so they can tap into their intuition quickly, translate what they receive accurately, and discern what's best for themselves and their businesses with confidence and ease. Learn more about her services at www.LeeMurphyWolf.com.

Carrie Wooden, Joy Coach, works with women who feel stuck, overwhelmed, frustrated, and generally burned out–to the point where they have forgotten how to dream, desire, and find the Joy and passion in their lives! Through her coaching, she supports women in overcoming overwhelm and burnout, to create a joy-filled purpose-driven life for themselves. Carrie is a certified Desire Factor Coach, Master certified QSCA Law of Attraction Coach, certified Ho'oponopono practitioner, SFT practitioner, life-long learner, and author. Learn more at www.CarrieWooden.com.

ABOUT THE PUBLISHER

About Our Publisher

LINDA JOY & INSPIRED LIVING PUBLISHING

*F*ounded in 2010 by Sacred Visibility™ Catalyst, Mindset Mojo™ Mentor, Intentional Living Guide™, radio show host, and Aspire Magazine Publisher Linda Joy, Inspired Living Publishing, LLC. (ILP), is a respected boutique hybrid publishing company.

Dedicated to publishing books for women and by women and to spreading a message of love, positivity, feminine wisdom, and self-empowerment to women of all ages, backgrounds, and life paths–Inspired Living Publishing's books have reached numerous international best-seller lists as well as Amazon's Movers & Shakers lists.

The company's authors benefit from Linda's family of multimedia inspirational brands that reach over 44,000 subscribers and social media community.

Inspired Living Publishing works with mission-driven, heart-centered female entrepreneurs–life, business and spiritual coaches, therapists, service providers, and health

163

practitioners in the personal and spiritual development genres, to bring their message and mission to life and to the world.

Through Inspired Living Publishing's highly successful sacred anthology division, hundreds of visionary female entrepreneurs have written their sacred soul stories using ILP's Authentic Storytelling™ writing model and became bestselling authors.

What sets Inspired Living Publishing™ apart is the powerful, high-visibility publishing, marketing, bestseller launch, and exposure across multiple media platforms that are included in its publishing packages. Their family of authors reap the benefits of being a part of a sacred family of inspirational multimedia brands that deliver the best in transformational and empowering content across a wide range of platforms.

Linda also works privately with empowered female entrepreneurs and messengers through her Illuminate Sistermind™ Program and other visibility-enhancing offerings. Linda's other visibility-enhancing brands including Inspired Living Secrets™, Inspired Living Giveaway™ and her popular radio show, Inspired Conversations.

Learn more about Linda's private work and offerings at **www.Linda-Joy.com**.

If you're ready to publish your transformational book or share your story in one of ours, we invite you to join us! Learn more about our publishing services at **InspiredLiving-Publishing.com.**

About Our Editor

DEBORAH KEVIN

As the founder and chief inspiration officer of Highlander Press, Deborah Kevin (pronounced "KEY-vin") loves helping change-makers tap into and share their stories of healing and truth with impactful books. She's trekked over 350 miles of the Camino de Santiago and her passions include travel, cooking, hiking, and kayaking. She lives in Maryland with the love of her life, Rob, her sons, and their puppy Fergus–that is when they're not off discovering the world. Learn more at www.DeborahKevin.com.

About Our Editor

JILL CELESTE

*J*ill Celeste, MA, loves Loud Women and loud bassets. That's why you will likely find her teaching marketing and mindset to female entrepreneurs at Celestial University; or facilitating sisterhood and connection through her online networking organization, Virtual Networkers; or hanging out with basset hounds as the co-founder of Tampa Bay Basset Hounds.

She lives near Tampa, Florida, with her husband, two sons, two cats, and a basset hound named Trixie. To learn more about Jill, please visit JillCeleste.com.

Inspired Living Publishing ~ Transforming Women's Lives, One Story at a Time™

If you enjoyed this book, visit
www.InspiredLivingPublishing.com
and sign up for ILP's e-zine to receive news about hot new releases,
promotions, and information on exciting author events.

Made in the USA
Las Vegas, NV
05 December 2022

60991231R00105